ALL THE SH!T

40 Lessons Learned from Making Mistakes

JOSEF CAUCHI

ALL THE SH!T
40 Lessons Learned from Making Mistakes

First Edition.

Contents

Introduction

Four decades ago, a miraculous event occurred. I took my first breath and was brought into this world. From the vast emptiness and nonexistence that I had known for an eternity before, I suddenly came to be. Alive. Aware.

The same wondrous event happened to you.

The same thing happened to billions of others before us. It's truly mind-blowing. And yet, this miracle happens every single day. It is estimated that three babies are born every second. Every second three human beings start their journey into this world, this reality. How will they spend their time on Earth? How long will they last? How did they come into existence now? Where were they for billions of years before today? When you stop to truly ponder on this fact, it becomes an awe-inspiring realization.

Where were we when dinosaurs roamed the Earth for millions of years? Where were we during the reign of the Roman Empire, when Europe ruled over much of the known world? Where were we when Columbus set sail for America and opened a new continent to the rest of the world? Where were we five years before we were born?

Perhaps we were just a mere thought in our parents' minds at the time. Or maybe it was all just a random occurrence in the grand scheme of things. One thing is certain though, at some point we came alive and began our journey to understand this game called life.

And that is what this book is all about - navigating through this dimension, this space, this game that we have been thrown into without any instructions or rulebook. We spend the first decade or so of our lives learning from our parents and teachers, and through our own experiences and mistakes. But once we reach adulthood, things become more complicated and unpredictable. We let go of the training wheels and are free to make bigger mistakes and face even greater challenges. In other words, we have to figure our shit out.

Every day, through every interaction and action, we learn more about how to play this game called adult life. We repeat our mistakes until finally, hopefully, we learn the lesson and store it in our minds for future reference. Sometimes events bring back memories of lessons our parents tried to teach us, but sometimes we realize that they were wrong, and we must find our own way. Because ultimately, we are all imperfect in this game where the end goal is uncertain, and all we truly want is to find happiness and contentment in this short time we have been given.

This book is a compilation of lessons I have learned throughout my life, after experiencing countless failures and mistakes. As a self-reflective individual, I often pause to try and make sense of my experiences and understand how the world works. I write down these lessons as a way to remember them, even though many of my notes have been lost over time.

I don't claim to have all the answers or lessons - far from it. I have only scratched the surface of what life has to offer and there is still so much more for me to learn. But through my own experiences, I do have some answers that I wish to share with you. I want to share with you the diamonds I found in the shit.

Why do I want to share this with you?

Because I believe that despite our individual realities, cultures, upbringings, and challenges, we are all bound by the limitations of our human bodies, and this shared reality. Whether rich or poor, ugly or beautiful, tall or short, we are all slaves to mortality. I had the pleasure of working for over a decade at an international company with people from diverse cultures and backgrounds. It became crystal clear that we all share a common yearning for happiness, care, good health, safety, fulfillment, personal growth, and love.

So, let us begin. Forty lessons for the forty years I have roamed this world.

But I ask one thing from you: do not simply binge-read each lesson without taking time to reflect on its meaning. For true understanding comes when we apply it to our own lives and experiences. If a lesson resonates with you or brings back memories of past growth and learning, take note of it! Circle it, highlight it, jot it down, or even tattoo it as a permanent reminder. The key is to never forget its importance.

These lessons have the power to change your life! They are a roadmap to better understand ourselves and our place in this reality. So please, take these words to heart and may they guide you on your journey towards fulfillment and growth.

40 LESSONS

1.

NO RISK, NO SPICE, NO LIFE.

The Comfort Zone. It is like a cozy cocoon where we feel at home. It is a peaceful place, offering a sense of control and predictability in our daily lives. There are rarely any big wins, but there is a general feeling of contentment. We may be happy for a while, or longer. But eventually, the need for something different arises - a new experience outside of the comfort bubble; something challenging that helps us grow and adds variety or meaning or sense to our life. We may be happy but not content.

But more often than not, we retreat back to our cozy sofa, back into the familiar comforts of our cocoon and wonder what could have been if we had taken that leap into the unknown, in the uncharted. There is little chance of feeling any new pain on the sofa, but there is also no room for new experiences and exciting possibilities.

Maybe we should get off the sofa.

However, that damn fear of the unknown strikes again. The fear that we will be worse off if we go for that new job opportunity, leave our home country behind, get married, attend that party, have a baby, audition for that role we've always wanted, ask out the person we fancy, or write that book we've been dreaming about. All because we are afraid of the potential negative consequences if things don't go as planned. "What if I fuck it up? What if it doesn't work?". So, we come up with excuses and think to ourselves "I just dodged a bullet there. It would have been too painful." And we remain in our safe zone. On our sofa, hugging our cushion and wondering.

Well, yes, it could have been painful. Going outside our comfort zone is never easy. But guess what - it could have also turned out positive as well. We could have gone on that date and found love. We could have aced that audition and landed our dream role. We could have made new friends who share our interests in a new country. We could have changed our lives for the better.

But we will never know.

Out of all the lessons in this book, I believe this is the one that I have struggled with the most and still struggle with every day. I often fear failure or looking foolish or ending up worse than I am now. "What if I end up earning less after I do this?". "What will my parents think of me if I go for this?". Perhaps as I get older, I care less about what others think, but for most of my life, I have been anchored in my comfort zone. I can recall many moments where anxiety dominated my nights and robbed me of sleep.

Back when I was a kid, I loved playing football (or soccer, as some call it). I love the game and watch countless matches on TV. My mother asked me if I wanted to join the local youth football (soccer) nursery, but I told her I didn't want to go. But did I really? Honestly, I was torn. Part of me yearned to be the next Messi, Del Piero or Ronaldo, weaving magic on the pitch. But the other part trembled at the thought of playing poorly and being ignored by other kids. I was so scared of failing and looking like an idiot. Many times, I wondered how I would have fared had I laced my football shoes, got onto that pitch and started training.

In my late teens, I often chickened out of meeting with my friends on weekends because I feared not having fun or feeling socially awkward around girls or not being good looking enough. But ironically, whenever I did find courage to go out, I always had a good time.

Throughout most of my work life, I rarely spoke up to management about my salary or work conditions or any office issues because I was afraid of appearing ungrateful or making things worse.

Even writing this very book was a daunting task for me. For a long time, I believed that my English wasn't strong enough (and it probably still isn't) or that I would never have enough material to write an entire book. I am no psychologist or guru or expert. I'm just a thinker. So, I shelved this dream. However, if you're reading this now, it's because I finally mustered up the courage to publish this book.

The thought often crosses my mind – what if I had embraced the unknown? Would my life have turned out differently? Perhaps I would have pursued a career in football, created more unforgettable teenage memories, or landed a higher paying job. These thoughts don't haunt me as strong regrets; rather, I see them as valuable lessons that shaped who I am today. They were necessary steps in my personal growth.

I share these stories with you because I want you to have more courage when facing the unknown. It's like a blank canvas full of endless adventures and opportunities waiting to be explored. And trust me, it's far better than clinging to your old familiar canvas.

Let's do an exercise together.

Remember the best moments of your life so far.

Was it the birth of your child, a first date with your spouse, achieving first place in a marathon, landing that new job, opening your business, moving to a new country or finally taking that trip of a lifetime? Now think about all the days and years leading up to that moment. More often than not, those incredible moments were the result of taking risks (big or small), making sacrifices, and stepping out of your comfort zone. You had to overcome challenges and face the fear of the unknown. This is often the path towards significant achievements – they require struggle, determination, endurance, and hard work.

In a world obsessed with instant gratification, the truth is that the best rewards in our journey were the result of deciding to dive into the uncomfortable and taking a risk that could have gone wrong.

Take a moment to reflect on this and hold onto this insight. Find the courage to try to embrace the unknown and all the possibilities it holds for your future self.

2.

COMPARISON: THE ULTIMATE HAPPINESS KILLER

Picture two young girls in the same kindergarten class. One receives a Pokémon school bag for her birthday, while the other watches with envy. The school bag is full of vibrant colors and features a cute little Pikachu. She asks her mother if she can have a Pokémon school bag too for her birthday but is denied because her current bag is still perfectly functional and looks new. The girl is filled with frustration and tears as she sees her classmate proudly displaying her prized possession. This simple and common example illustrates how early in life we begin to compare ourselves to others and feel a sense of imbalance.

Comparison is like poison.

We constantly scan those around us and highlight our own shortcomings in comparison to the strengths and possessions of other people. Instead of focusing on the abundance of blessings in our lives - like having a roof over our head, food to eat, our health, a loving family and a good standard of living - we fixate on what we lack in comparison to others. We become obsessed with how unfair life seems when we see our colleague get promoted, our neighbor wins the lottery, or the popular kid at school who seems to have everything handed to them on a silver platter. And in turn, we become sad or bitter and start to blame factors like our DNA, family, luck, or fate.

"Damn it! My life sucks!" we say as we compare ourselves with everyone else who seems to have it together.

Envy - that potent and destructive emotion that can consume us and drive us to do things we wouldn't normally do. It's a fire that burns hot, fueled by our own insecurities and desires.

I am also a victim of this envy trap. In fact, I have fallen prey to its grip many times before. As a teenager, I fell often into the trap of comparing myself to other teenagers. They all seemed to be extroverted and confident. They all seemed to have sculpted physiques, captivating good looks, and effortless charm, which left me feeling down.

In my 20s when I found myself bitter and resentful of the success of some friends who had taken risks to start their own businesses, were in a loving relationship or traveled often. I was single, earning little money and mostly bound to the island of Malta. It consumed me, this burning desire to escape the 9-5 job and achieve the same level of success as those guys. I worked tirelessly during the night on my online side hustles, often neglecting my well-being (especially sleep) and family, all in pursuit of the goal: to have the same success as others. But in reality, my current job was stable and stress-free, a fortunate position that I failed to fully appreciate. I also had a great group of friends and an amazing family. Instead, I compared myself constantly to one particular individual who seemed to have it all. He had the perfect life - or that's what I thought. Looking back now, I realize that I should have used my time to truly reflect on my blessings and use my energy to pursue my true passions instead of wasting time comparing myself, feeling sorry for myself, imitating other people and chasing after something that ultimately left me feeling empty and exhausted, like a wild animal constantly searching for food.

A thought I have heard and has stuck with me since is the fact that at this moment in time there are millions worse off than us. Many people crave a job, a safe place to live, or even the ability to read. According to a 2023 UN report, over 700 million people worldwide can't read or write. The same report estimates one-quarter of the world doesn't have access to clean water. That's 2 billion people unsure whether the water they're drinking is safe or not!

That doesn't negate your own struggles. You've clearly been through something difficult, and my condolences for that. It's likely others have faced similar hardships, but that doesn't diminish your own experience.

It may be hard to hear, but the reality is that no one is perfect and there will ALWAYS be people who are better than us at something or in a better state than us. Fact. But instead of getting caught up in this cycle of comparison and envy, we should shift our focus to the only person we should compare ourselves to. And that is … us. Progress and personal growth come from understanding ourselves, accepting our flaws, and working towards becoming a better version of ourselves. We cannot change everything about ourselves, but we can choose to embrace our imperfections and strive for improvement where possible. This is the path to self-love and true happiness.

Don't compare yourself to others if you want happiness. Social media portrays a highlight reel, showcasing only the best moments while concealing struggles and insecurities. You have no idea what someone else is truly going through.

Instead, focus on yourself. Appreciate what you have, cultivate gratitude, and set new goals for personal growth.

That being said…

… it's perfectly okay to be inspired by others. Inspiration can be a powerful motivator. If you admire someone's accomplishments, their approach to challenges, or their work ethic, that's fantastic! The key is to use that inspiration to fuel your own motivation and take action, not to compare yourself to them and feel discouraged.

A great example for me is American filmmaker Robert Rodriguez, known for the Spy Kids movies and the El Mariachi trilogy. His book "Rebel Without a Crew" details the incredible challenges he faced in funding and directing his first movie. His dedication was so strong that he even signed up for medical experiments to raise money for his film. Reading about his journey was incredibly inspiring – his drive and grit really motivated me. Now, hold on a minute! I didn't exactly follow in his footsteps and sign up for medical tests to raise money for my films. What I did instead was start writing my own short films and filming them with the least money possible. So, Robert, if you're reading this, thanks for inspiring me.

So please utilize your time and energy in the best way. Comparison makes us feel inferior and bad. Inspiration helps us act without destroying our self-worth.

3.

PLEASING EVERYONE? RECIPE FOR MISERY

As social creatures, humans strive for love, harmony, and acceptance. We long to be on good terms with those around us, both friends and strangers alike. And yet, in our pursuit of maintaining this harmonious environment, we often fall into the trap of trying to make everyone happy. But this is an impossible task. It's draining, time-consuming, and ultimately dangerous as we give away control of our own happiness.

Have you ever found yourself feeling sad because of one person's disapproval, despite being surrounded by a loving family and close friends? It's a common dilemma - putting too much weight on the opinions of others who may not truly matter in our lives. I know this all too well from my own journey on this planet. For years, I tried to please everyone, even those who treated me poorly. I played the role of a chameleon, constantly changing myself to fit in and gain more "friends". I said yes to events I didn't want to attend and suppressed my own thoughts and values out of fear of rejection. I agreed with everyone about everything. I was the guy without an opinion.

The result? Stress, burnout, loss of self-identity, and depression. And at the end of it all, most of these friendships were shallow and inauthentic. Looking back, I realize I should have focused my energy on building deeper connections with those few who genuinely cared about me.

You see, no matter how hard we try, there will always be someone who is unhappy with us. The key is to be true to ourselves and stand by our values. Learning to say no with respect and honesty is crucial in preserving our own well-being. "I'm sorry, but not this time," should suffice.

We often spend too much time analyzing others' reactions to us instead of prioritizing our own thoughts, feelings, and happiness. We place too much weight on how others perceive us. Of course, we should care about how others feel but not at the expense of neglecting our own needs.

In the end, our own validation is what truly matters.

So let go of the need to make everyone happy and focus on your own journey towards contentment and self-acceptance.

4.

STUMBLE, LEARN, WIN, REPEAT.

Failures are a major part of the game, though we often avoid them at all costs.

Let's be honest: Failing is not a pleasant experience. Failing sucks. It makes us feel foolish and weak, forcing us to confront our own insecurities and shortcomings. We strive for consistency and excellence, dreaming of being winners and achieving greatness. We yearn for a better future - whether it be a dream job or taking steps towards our goals. Yet, in our pursuit of success, we tend to choose the safest path with the least risk of failure or mistakes. And so, we often do nothing at all, staying stale in our comfort zone. And in doing so, we miss out on growth and opportunity.

Here's the truth: failure is an essential part of the journey. It's the ultimate teacher, the king, the GOAT (greatest of all time). Let's look at some examples.

Roger Federer, a tennis legend with a record-breaking 20 Grand Slam titles, wasn't always consistent. Early in his career, emotional outbursts and anger led to frequent losses. However, he learned to control his emotions and turned those defeats into lessons. Today, he's one of the best tennis players ever.

Similarly, basketball legend Michael Jordan famously got cut from his high school basketball team. But rejection didn't stop him. He used it as fuel, pushing himself harder to become the most decorated and recognizable basketball player of all time.

Both could have easily given up at some point. You can argue that failure made them legends. They had to face setbacks in order for them to learn their lessons and push harder.

For some years I've attempted selling products online that no one bought, made short films that were pretty bad, launched blogs with barely any views, stumbled through presentations at work, and even dented my first car multiple times in the first few months of driving it.

But each failure taught me valuable lessons. I learned what not to do next time, how to improve, and how to approach things differently. Sometimes, I even discovered that certain pursuits were not meant for me. And that's okay. In fact, giving up certain things can be a valuable lesson in itself. But if you truly, honestly want to pursue something that means a lot to you, then giving up should be the last thing that comes to your mind. You have to be like Jordan.

So why is failure the protagonist in our learning journey? Why isn't it school or university, or books or learning from others? Because the best way to truly learn anything is by experiencing it ourselves - attempting the entire process and inevitably encountering failures along the way. As much as teachers or books or external sources can guide us, it is ultimately up to us to act and learn from our own experiences.

In conclusion, it's okay to fail, as long as we keep trying and learning from our mistakes. It may sound unbelievable, but every mistake can actually be seen as a step forward if you take the time to reflect on it and learn from it.

The avoidance of failures IS NOT a measure of success. So don't be afraid to take risks and embrace failures as opportunities for growth.

5.

DON'T TAKE LIFE TOO SERIOUSLY

One of the most beloved quotes I've ever encountered is by the American writer Elbert Hubbard: "Don't take life too seriously. You will never get out of it alive." It's a brilliantly humorous and penetrating reminder that life is meant to be lived with lightness and joy, not with excessive seriousness. I would like to highlight the words "too seriously" from the quote. There still needs to be a balance in how we approach life's challenges.

Life is not a joke. Far from it. Life is the greatest and most mysterious thing we have been given, and we will ever have. We were nothing before and suddenly we had a chance to experience all of this, to live and breathe in a world where the answers are elusive. It's a world that can be scary at times and very challenging.

As someone who has struggled with anxiety for much of my adult life, I often found myself consumed by thoughts of what could go wrong. Whether it was worrying about an upcoming exam or a simple complaint to a handyman, my mind would race through every possible scenario and prepare for all potential reactions. Looking back now, I realize that 99% of these imagined scenarios never actually came to fruition. Anxiety is truly a draining and irrational force.

Stoic philosopher Seneca once said, "We suffer more often in imagination than in reality." And when you begin to loosen your grip on life and its seriousness, you come to understand that these worries and fears will likely mean nothing in five years' time. Problems will always arise, but you learn to deal with them as they come without overthinking or being overly focused on them. Life should not be one long marathon of responsibilities and duties - it's about finding joy and laughter along the way without fear of judgment. We should not allow fear and anxiety to suck the joy from our life.

Take dancing at a party for example - so many people avoid it because they fear looking foolish. But look around, everyone is already having silly fun. Might as well join in on the quirky carnival that is life.

And don't forget to laugh. Humor can provide a temporary reprieve from negative feelings and even jumpstart the healing process. Life doesn't have to be serious and heavy all the time - laughter can help you destress, open your heart, connect with others, and shift the narrative of your life. Throughout my life, I always found that humor brings people together and brightens the air.

"But how can I laugh or be happy? DO YOU KNOW what happened to me?"

You are right. Life is certainly not easy, and there will be times when it feels unbearably hard. My suggestion to take life less seriously does not mean to disregard your emotions, but to start the journey of accepting what happened and start the recovery. In time you will find a way to add more joy - you find a way to smile. My suggestion is to get closer to people who fill you with joy, humor and love for life.

People sometimes comment on how positive I am, or how quickly I move on from serious topics. That's true. I dislike drama and find it draining when people dwell on negative experiences. I also prefer not to surround myself with people who are constantly serious or fixated on potential problems. These individuals aren't much fun to be around.

I already experience anxiety and don't need additional reasons to feel stressed or worried. While I understand the importance of addressing serious matters, I also need to prioritize joy, laughter, and gratitude for the good things in my life. Over time, I've found that many people share this mindset, and I naturally gravitate towards them.

In conclusion, don't be like Grumpy from Snow White. His constant seriousness and complaining likely prevented him from enjoying life as much as the other dwarfs.

As a bonus to this lesson, I have to end this chapter with a few cheesy jokes. I apologize in advance for this page. Brace yourselves!

I told my wife she was drawing her eyebrows too high. She looked surprised.

What's a skeleton's least favorite room in the house?
The living room.

I asked my dad for his best dad joke, and he said, 'You.'

Have you heard of a new restaurant called Karma?
There's no menu: You get what you deserve.

I told my wife she should embrace her mistakes.
She gave me a hug.

What did one plate say to another?
"Lunch is on me."

And a Chuck Norris fact to end it all. Chuck Norris once got bitten by a king cobra. After 3 days of excruciating pain… the cobra died.

"Life is short. Smile while you still have teeth." - Mallory Hopkins

6.

LOVE YOUR CARDS. PLAY YOUR BEST GAME.

The biggest challenge that you are going to face in life is how to find contentment and happiness, even with all your imperfections and all the challenges you face.

Let's be real - none of us are perfect.

Not you, not me, not your family, not your friends, not your chihuahua, not your goldfish, not even the celebrities we idolize. We all have our flaws and struggles. Perhaps you have a disability or a difficult personality. Maybe you are vertically challenged (short) or have weaker teeth than most. You might battle constant fear or envy or anxiety. You could even exhibit narcissistic or overly positive behavior. Mental illness may be a part of your daily life, or perhaps you just struggle with self-image. Your background could include growing up as an orphan or having parents who divorced when you were young. You might have difficulty focusing or suffer from gluten intolerance. In other words, there are aspects of ourselves that are less than ideal.

And then there are moments in life where these imperfections seem to take center stage, leaving us feeling even more like shit. Maybe a bully targets you because of your appearance. Or you lose a job due to an outburst of anger. Or your wheelchair prevents you from joining your friends on a field trip. Or your social awkwardness prevents you from finding a romantic partner. These experiences can leave us feeling sad, depressed, and resentful towards our lives and circumstances.

It's understandable to feel this way - it's not fair that we weren't dealt a better hand in life, especially when others around us seem to have it easier. But here's the thing, what are you going to do about it? We have two options when faced with this reality. Option one is to spend our days wallowing in self-pity and dragging ourselves through life. What a waste! Option two is to accept the cards we've been dealt, count our blessings and strengths, and make the best play we can with what we have.

We have to play the best game with the cards we were given.

So what does that mean? Instead of fixating on what we lack, let's focus on what we do have. Are you intelligent? Use that to learn, study, teach, and create a better life for yourself. Are you creative? Express yourself through art, design, or experimentation. Are you empathetic? Use your compassion to help others in need. Are you a loving person? Cultivate meaningful relationships and spread love wherever you go. Are you athletic? Push your physical limits, challenge yourself, and connect with others who share your passion. In short, go out and conquer the world. You are more than the sum of your imperfections and failures. Don't waste your energy crying and feeling sorry for yourself - instead, use it to make the most of your talents and life experiences. You are not just "John, the guy in the wheelchair" - you are John, an incredible individual with unique skills and potential.

I am far from perfect. I am packing on some extra weight lately. I had acne for a long while. I am yeast intolerant and cannot eat pizza and drink wine or beer. My beard was white before my 40. And then there are the mysterious results from my blood tests, hinting at liver issues that could derail everything. I get tonsillitis every six months. Anxiety and a tendency to leave things unfinished are just a couple more of the many cards stacked against me, causing countless moments of despair.

As I'm typing this, a flashback hits me. I'm back at a pool as a teenager, the only one wearing a t-shirt over my swimsuit. That summer, my back acne was so bad... Why did it hit me so hard when everyone else seemed flawless?

But amidst all these struggles, I have some good cards too. I take pride in my smart, introspective nature and genuine concern for others' emotions. There's also a dash of creativity and humor thrown into the mix. Over time, I've learned to shift my focus from dwelling on my flaws to embracing and nurturing my strengths. This mindset has allowed me to accept myself as I am and move forward with courage.

I started losing hair before anyone else in my university class. While others worried about exams and dating, I obsessed over hiding my receding hairline. Creams, foams, shampoos - nothing could stop the inevitable. Eventually, in my late 20s, I made the decision to embrace my baldness and shaved off what little hair remained. The initial reactions from those around me ranged from confusion to pity, but eventually they got used to the new bald-headed Josef. And if they didn't like it? Well, I learned that their opinions don't define me.

The greatest challenge in life is learning to love yourself despite your imperfections. So often, we rely on the love and approval of others before granting ourselves the same kindness. But true self-acceptance and self-love can only come from within.

Only when we believe in and love ourselves can we truly thrive, regardless of what others may think.

7.

SURROUND YOURSELF WITH GOOD PEOPLE

Good people, good life.

This is one of the lessons we all learn in life, one way or another. Had I learned this early in my life it would have saved me an immense amount of trouble, anxiety, and time. It may seem like an obvious statement, but it's one that is often overlooked by many children as they grow up. If only when we are young we are not lured by the people on the dark side, it could prevent so much suffering.

I know this may sound extreme, but I firmly believe it: there are some truly bad people in the world. People who take pleasure in seeing others suffer or being cruel to them without a second thought. Can you think of a few? I know a dozen. Of course, nobody is purely good or evil, but some individuals come close to being on that dark end of the spectrum. And when you add up all their traits and actions, they ultimately bring more negativity than positivity into our lives. These are the kinds of people we should distance ourselves from and not allow them to be part of our life story.

But unfortunately, even though we know we should avoid these people, sometimes we still find ourselves in their presence. We normalize their harmful behavior and simply accept that this is how things are. We stay in toxic relationships or social groups where bullies continue to belittle us, or we remain in jobs where we are constantly mistreated. Why do we do this? Sometimes it's because we lack the energy or motivation to leave these negative situations behind, knowing that doing so might also mean leaving behind good people. But here's the thing - you never know what awaits you on the other side until you take a leap of faith. Many people have cut ties with toxic individuals or left unhealthy environments and found themselves feeling revitalized and truly living again.

There's a saying that "proximity is power". This means that the people we surround ourselves with can greatly influence us and shape who we become over time. So it's important to choose wisely and stay close to those whose values or skills we admire. Take a moment to reflect on this statement: who do you currently surround yourself with? Is there any toxic, negative, or abusive individual in your life that may eventually start to affect your own behavior? It's crucial to distance ourselves from these people and instead gravitate towards those who are positive, kind, and encouraging. By doing so, we not only become better individuals ourselves, but we also help others grow and improve.

If you surround yourself with shit, you will start smelling like shit!

I admit I haven't always chosen the best friends. In my teenage years especially, some of my friendships negatively influenced my behavior and thinking.

At sixteen, I befriended two arrogant guys at college for a month or so. Their confidence, seemingly carefree attitude, and the fact that they never seemed to pick on me drew me in. One day, we were at a grocery store near school, buying snacks. After paying, we were waiting by the door for our other friend. The guys next to me whispered, suggesting we could easily steal something since the shopkeeper wasn't looking. He grabbed a large soda and ran out as fast as he could. Without thinking clearly, I grabbed two more bottles and followed him outside. I grabbed two to impress, wanting to fit in, I suppose. The other friend joined us later, thrilled with our "badass" act of stealing three sodas.

However, as we finished the drinks and walked to the college bathrooms, I started feeling guilty. My conscience started working again. This wasn't who I was! What the fuck was I doing hanging out with these guys? They wanted to repeat the stunt, but I knew I had to distance myself from these guys, and so I did.

Fortunately, I've been lucky enough to make friends with some truly wonderful and kind people throughout my life. While I know a lot of people, I have a select few close friends who share my core values. While they may not share all my interests, they are the best people I know.

I believe that before we can attract new positive influences into our lives, we must first self-reflect and identify what values and interests are important to us. Then, we can start expanding our circle to include new people, environments, ideas, relationships, and friendships. You never know, you might find your soul mate in this new expanded circle! Someone that shares your values.

Remember, it's quality over quantity. Surrounding ourselves with good people will ultimately lead us down a happier and brighter path in life.

8.

GOALS WITHOUT A PLAN ARE JUST DREAMS

Dreams. What a beautiful word. The possibility of a future situation where everything is better, where all your wishes and desires come true. But then you wake up from your daydreaming, the dream fades away like mist in the morning, and you are left with the bitter taste of reality. Should dreams just be a fleeting moment of escapism?

No, they should not be. Dreams should be our fuel, our motivation to transform them into reality. We need to take action and make them materialize. So what should we do?

We need a plan.

We cannot simply wait for an opportunity to knock on our door and hand us success on a silver platter. No, we must go out and work towards our dreams. And while the word "plan" may sound daunting, it simply means coming up with the next step to get closer to our goal and actually taking action towards it.

And we can also support our friends in their dreams. When your friend brings up the usual "Bro, one day I would like to do [insert dream]", you should follow that with "So what are you doing about it?"

As a child, I would often lie on a low wall at school, gazing up at the magnificent clouds drifting across the blue sky. Some remained still, while others moved fast in the wind, some big and some tiny. They reminded me of dreams, perhaps because of their resemblance to fluffy cotton, like soft beds. Some clouds were vast and static, mirroring big dreams that we can't let go, while others disappeared like fleeting wishes. Each dream, a unique shape and size. I often wondered which of my dreams would one day come true.

Let's turn our dreams into concrete goals and take the first step towards achieving them. It's always helpful to break down big goals into smaller, manageable steps that align with your dream. Here are a few examples:

If you dream of playing in a rock band but don't know how to play an instrument, schedule your first guitar lesson today.

If you want to reconcile with your estranged son, put your pride aside, reach out to him, and suggest meeting for coffee.

To lose weight, find a nutritionist or join a gym. Search online for one in your area and make an appointment now.

To find love, start attending events related to your hobbies or interests. You might meet someone who shares your passions. You can also try downloading a dating app.

If you want to leave your job, start by defining the kind of job you want and actively search for opportunities in that field.

For those dreaming of migrating to another country, create a list of the costs and challenges involved and start making plans to overcome them.

If writing a book is your dream, open a blank document and start writing the first page.

If you aspire to become rich, research different paths to wealth and focus on one that suits you. Write down your plan and set a deadline for your first step.

Don't wait! Take that first step within the next hour.

Daydreaming will not get us any closer to our goals. Let's act and make our dreams come true. It's time to figure out the next step and go for it!

9.

SHYNESS
=
MISSED
CHANCES

Shyness and fear are two powerful emotions that can hold us back from seizing opportunities in life.

I remember when I was just 14 years old, my mother told me about a youth center in our town where kids my age gather to organize and act in theater plays. She wanted me to get out of the house and make new friends instead of spending all day playing video games on my trusty Pentium computer. The thought of meeting new people excited me, especially since this center was only a 10-minute walk away from my house. But as I stood in front of the slightly ajar door, laughter could be heard from inside. And I froze. My shyness took over, and I couldn't bring myself to step inside. What if they didn't like me? What if I didn't fit in? Those thoughts consumed me, and I turned around and went back home, making up some excuse to my mother for why I returned so quickly.

Looking back, it may seem like a small moment, but it affected me deeply. If only I had mustered the courage to walk through that door, I might have made new friends and experienced things like being part of a play or organizing events. But my shyness and fear held me back from the unknown.

Eventually, with time, I had to overcome my shyness. It was hindering me from gaining new experiences and living life to the fullest. Shyness is not necessarily a bad trait - introverts thrive in their solitude - but for me, it was more about insecurity and fear of interaction. It fed me self-doubt and caution, hindering my ability to fully embrace social interactions in this world built on connections.

But slowly, I learned to put less weight on what others might think or do, to stop being paralyzed by fear and instead focus on curiosity rather than worry. If only I had chosen happiness over fear, I could have walked through that door and accepted whatever life had in store for me. Instead, my choice to give up on that opportunity left me feeling miserable.

I now realize that opportunities often come disguised as discomfort. It takes courage to push past our fears and take a leap into the unknown. And while being brave doesn't mean you have no fear, it means suppressing that feeling and taking a chance.

I believe overcoming shyness isn't like flipping a switch; it doesn't disappear overnight. It's more of a gradual journey, one step forward at a time. It can start with a simple conversation with someone you barely know, or by complimenting a stranger. This is what they call a gradual exposure to uncomfortable social situations. Start small with a simple conversation every day or at least a smile.

What helped me was suppressing negative thoughts – all the worries about things going wrong. I remember clenching my fist, saying "fuck it," and diving headfirst into uncomfortable situations. I didn't need to make everyone like me. I understood that awkwardness was not the end of the world. I understood that my past mistakes did not mean I will repeat them again. I realized we are all imperfect in an imperfect world.

Over time, those situations became less uncomfortable, and I felt myself growing… evolving. In time I have learned to not let my worries of social interaction get in the way of opportunities that present themselves.

In the end, opportunities favor the brave - those who choose to face their fears and embrace the unknown with open arms.

10.

DON'T TILT.
BALANCE
IS
KEY

The phrase "balance is key" seems to always find its way into my daily conversations, as I strive to achieve equilibrium in various aspects of life. But what exactly does it mean? To me, it means finding harmony by carefully managing and balancing different elements without giving too much weight to one side. These elements can range from work and leisure, physical and mental health, family and friends, career and children, etc. It's about recognizing that putting all your energy into one thing will inevitably cause other areas of your life to suffer.

One common example is the concept of "work-life balance." While aiming for a successful career is admirable, it should not come at the expense of neglecting your family or personal well-being. On the other hand, solely focusing on your loved ones may cause missed opportunities for career growth. It's crucial to find a healthy balance between these two important aspects of life.

Another area where balance is essential is relationships. While investing time and effort into making your partner happy is important, it's also crucial to prioritize taking care of yourself and pursuing your own dreams. Neglecting either aspect can lead to resentment and regret in the long run.

Even when it comes to diet and food choices, balance is key. Restricting yourself from indulging in your favorite foods may seem like the best way to stay healthy, but studies have shown that incorporating some treats into a balanced and nutritious diet, or finding a diet that strikes a good balance between taste and healthiness leads to better long-term commitment.

Let me ask you a question: What kind of person are you? Are you someone who's never content, constantly pushing themselves to grow and develop? Or are you someone who's happy with who they are, accepting themselves and not striving for more? In my opinion, we should balance these two types. We need to accept our failures, celebrate our wins, but still believe in our potential and push forward.

But how do we find this balance?

For me, it's all about priorities, compromises, and boundaries. As life constantly changes, so should our priorities. When I had children, they became my top priority, leading me to reevaluate my social life and set boundaries for myself in terms of work-life balance. This meant going out with friends less often than before and prioritizing playtime with my children over playing my video games.

I believe that it's an ongoing process of analyzing what is most important at any given moment and creating schedules, boundaries, and compromises accordingly.

If you care, you will find a way to balance things.

Although it may be challenging to find the perfect balance, it ultimately leads to a happier and healthier life. Tilting too much towards one side will only bring regret and imbalance. So remember, balance is key in creating a harmonious and fulfilling existence.

11.

GRIT FUELS MIGHT

Let me tell you a story about a man I once knew, whose determination and resilience left a lasting impression on me. His name was Mike (not his real name), and he had a decent job that allowed him to survive and even save up for a yearly holiday. But his true passion lay in photography - he dreamed of making it his career. So he bought himself a decent camera and started sharing his photos on social media.

But, if I'm being completely honest, Mike's photos were far from impressive. In fact, they were some of the worst I had ever seen on my social media feed. He lacked knowledge of framing subjects, creativity in his ideas, and had a tendency to overdo it with photo editing. Even though some people would "like" his photos, they were mostly just family and close friends. And every now and then, someone would drop a harsh but truthful comment about how bad his photos were.

I never commented on his photos myself, but deep down I always thought he should give up on this dream and pursue something else.

One day, to my surprise, Mike quit his full-time job and started a photography business. It seemed like the worst idea ever. I mean, his skills were clearly lacking and his previous attempts at photography had been cringeworthy at best. My friends would share with me his photos with captions like "Oh my god! This is so bad". This guy was doomed.

But despite all this, Mike persisted. He took photoshoots of happy couples before their weddings or expecting mothers posing on beaches with their bellies exposed. And let me tell you, those photos were still pretty shit.

Yet somehow, through all the setbacks and criticism from clients who didn't like his work, Mike remained driven and determined to make his dream a reality. And slowly but surely, I began to notice an improvement in the photos he shared on social media. The framing, mise-en-scene, and lighting were all getting better and better. His pitches and ideas were also improving. Eventually, he became so skilled and popular that the company I worked for even hired him to shoot a private event.

Mike recently opened a second shop in another part of the country, and it seems business is thriving. His success is a testament to his belief in himself and his refusal to give up. As for myself, I can think of several instances where I prematurely abandoned my goals after facing early challenges. The self-doubt would creep in, leading me to believe 'Maybe this isn't for me.' And sometimes I wonder what it would have been had I kept believing in myself.

I learned a valuable lesson from Mike - if you truly want something, you will find a way to make it happen. It doesn't matter if you have natural talent or luck on your side. With perseverance and belief in oneself, a lot of things you thought impossible become possible. Do note how I avoided saying "anything is possible" because that would not be the truth. Still you should not underestimate the power of grit and the things you can achieve with it.

And as I watched Mike achieve his dream through hard work and resilience, it reminded me that success isn't always about innate ability or training - sometimes it's simply about never giving up. It's about being bold.

And then, if you possess talent and combine it with determination, you have a potent combination. My brother Daniel exemplifies this perfectly. He has always been a gifted musician, proficient in playing the piano and various percussion instruments. At the age of 19, he established his 17-piece big band, which continues to thrive. Later, at the age of 27, he founded his arts school, which is also flourishing. Aside from his unwavering hard work, Daniel's success is attributed to his self-belief and willingness to take risks.

So don't give up yet. Keep fighting for your dreams.

12.

BE THE SUNSHINE, NOT THE SHADE

In every relationship, there will inevitably be conflicts that arise. It could be a simple disagreement that escalates out of control, or an accusation that is denied and leads to a standoff. These conflicts can often cause broken relationships, leaving both parties physically close but emotionally distant. However, I have learned throughout my life that to find harmony and peace, one of the two parties must rise above the conflict and be the better person.

But why should I make the effort if I was falsely accused or disrespected? Why should I try to mend things if the other person won't even take the first step? Why should I be the light when the other person chose the darkness?

Because you are the better person.

If you truly care about this relationship and want to see it thrive again, then you must set aside your ego and your desire to win and instead reach out to the other person. It may not be easy, and your efforts may be refused at first, but your heart will find solace in knowing that you tried to make amends. And who knows, it might just work. If it doesn't… well… you have tried.

Your small act of kindness and empathy could have a ripple effect and pave the way for a brighter future. You don't have to conform to societal norms; you can choose to be a better person.

Some may say that apologizing makes you appear weak or vulnerable. But I believe that a sincere apology shows maturity, empathy, and genuine concern for the other person's feelings. Of course, constantly apologizing without true remorse is a red flag. But a genuine apology can promote healing and restore trust between two individuals. We are all human and we all make mistakes; it takes both parties making an effort to become better people in order for healing to occur. However, someone must take the first step.

It's natural not to get along with everyone, especially those who are assholes or have been disrespectful to me in the past, like some of my rude colleagues. While I don't need to be best friends with everyone I meet, I also don't hold grudges or wish them any harm. If they approach me, I'll be polite and even try to maintain a positive attitude, even if we don't become friends. I believe in trying to be the better person. In my mind it feels like this is a better way than avoiding people or being constantly angry at others.

Choosing to be the better person is not an easy task, but it challenges us to become more patient, empathetic, mature, and ultimately more understanding.

In the end, it leads to growth and a better version of ourselves. A brighter version. One that illuminates a room and the people inside.

13.

BE GRATEFUL

"This is a glorious day," exclaimed the renowned American poet Maya Angelou. "I have never seen one quite like it before."

Take a moment to look at yourself. You are alive - breathing, reading, and experiencing life in all its complexities. It is a blessing that should not be taken for granted. Yes, there may be things you wish to change or complain about in your life, but if you focus all your energy on those negative aspects, you will only drag yourself down and make the day more difficult. Instead, focus on blessings and positives in your life. Not only will this bring positivity into your own day, but it can also spread to those around you.

I am not suggesting that you ignore what is wrong in your life, but it's all about your attitude towards it. Pain and problems will always exist, but facing them with determination and hope for a better future can make all the difference. And remember, sulking and complaining does not solve anything.

Need a reminder of how awesome your life truly is? Take a break from technology and grab an old-fashioned pen and paper. Write down a list of all the things you are grateful for in your life right now - whether it's people, possessions, opportunities or simple everyday things that bring joy and meaning to your life. Reflecting on these blessings can help paint a more realistic picture of your overall life, rather than just focusing on the negatives.

Do you feel more mindful of your life now? Can you see that it resembles a Yin Yang circle rather than a black hole? This lesson is about finding balance and appreciating the good while acknowledging and facing the bad. You must look beyond the shit.

One final point - I do not want to impose any religious beliefs onto you, but I must share this personal habit of mine. Every night before bed, as I lie in my bed looking up at the ceiling, I take a moment to think about all the wonderful things that happened to me that day. Even if it was a difficult or challenging day, I make an effort to find something positive that occurred during the day. And then I simply say "thanks" and end the day. To whom am I saying thanks? Is it to a higher power, God, the universe, or destiny? It is not for me to say, but it feels right and causes no harm. Take a chance and try it out for yourself.

Thanks.

14.

YOU CAN INFLUENCE BUT NOT CONTROL

From a young age, one of the most important lessons we learn is that there are many things in life that we cannot control. We have no power over how others act, the forces of nature, stock market fluctuations, the results of a sporting event or even how healthy you'll wake up tomorrow. It can be frustrating to realize this, but accepting it early on can save us from constant disappointment and anger when things don't go our way. Instead of fighting against what happens, we must learn to accept it and focus on how we react to these situations.

I remember being 16 and working as a waiter in a restaurant during the summer. I watched as one of the managers barked orders at us and expected us to follow them without question. At first, I thought being a manager must be the coolest job ever - being in charge, giving orders, and having control over others. But soon I saw that this type of control was not effective. People would slack off the moment the manager wasn't watching, everyone seemed to dislike the manager, employees were quitting after just a few weeks, and some tasks were left undone when the manager wasn't around. I realized that this manager could have been more successful if they had set an example for how to wait tables, listened to our ideas for improving service, helped us when needed, and allowed for some flexibility. Had they focused on influencing rather than controlling, we would have done a better job.

One skill that is crucial to develop is the power of influence. We all have the ability to inspire and persuade others, shape our days and the success of projects. While control can often be negative and direct, influence tends to be positive and indirect.

Let's look at some examples. Imagine you want to plan a trip to Rome with a friend - something you've been dreaming about for a long time. Sadly, your friend doesn't share your enthusiasm. Of course, you can't force them to come - you can't tie them up and stuff them in a suitcase hoping they'll survive the flight in the luggage compartment. So what can you do? You can try to influence or persuade them. How? The first step is simply listening. Ask your friend why they don't want to go. What is their real reason for not wanting to take this trip? After some probing, you discover that their hesitation is not due to a dislike of Rome or Italians, but because they are afraid of getting sick on long flights. You remind them of your last trip together which went smoothly. You show them videos of the beautiful sights in Rome - the Colosseum, the Trevi Fountain, and more. You also mention the motion sickness pills they took on the last flight that helped them get through it without any issues.

Your friend is convinced and you both end up having an amazing time in Rome.

This isn't about using manipulative mind games or trying to control others' thoughts and actions. It's about being proactive in our own lives and taking action to shape our experiences. To effectively influence the world around us, we must first understand it and what drives it, and then take action accordingly.

Let me tell you a story. This one is a fable and it is called The Wind and the Sun. As far as I know this is another gem from the Greek storyteller Aesop.

The Wind and Sun once argued over who was stronger. They saw a man wearing a thick coat and challenged each other on who would make the man remove his coat. The Wind puffed out its chest and blew a big gust at a man walking down the road. The man was cold and so he just held his coat tighter against the wind. The Wind blew harder and harder, but the man wouldn't budge.

Seeing this, the Sun smiled. It didn't blow at all, but instead sent down warm rays of light. The man felt the sunbeams on his face and started to feel a little warm. He loosened his coat a bit. The Sun kept shining gently, and soon the man felt too hot in his coat. He finally took it off completely and enjoyed the sunshine.

Most of the time, being kind and gentle, like the Sun, is better at influencing others, rather than using force or trying to control things, like the Wind.

15.

MARCH TO YOUR OWN DRUM

You do not need to follow the herd. You are not a sheep.

The pull to follow the herd is ingrained in our nature. An evolutionary advantage, it offers safety in numbers and requires less thinking. The comfort of knowing you are not alone if things go wrong can be tempting. In addition, there is a sense of social validation and belonging that comes with following the crowd. However, this behavior can also come at a cost.

The danger of succumbing to the desires and direction of the herd is that it can lead to suppressing your own feelings, desires, dreams, and even core values. This phenomenon, known as herd mentality, is particularly prevalent during adolescence.

During those formative years, we all feel the need to belong and will often shape our character and want to fit in with a group. I remember when I was a child, I prided myself on being a "good boy." I was respectful, empathetic, and always willing to help others. But one day, I witnessed a group of bullies harassing another boy. My heart went out to him, but when the leader of the bullies turned his attention on me, something inside me shifted. Fueled by my desire to fit in with them, I started insulting the same boy I had felt sorry for just moments before. The bullies found it hilarious, and for a while, I was part of their group led by Kevin (not his real name).

Despite knowing deep down that what I was doing was wrong, I managed to suppress my values and conscience to maintain my newfound place in the herd.

That all changed one day when another boy named Tony stood up to Kevin's bullying tactics. Tony was someone I looked up to - he was confident, popular and a great footballer. Seeing him bravely defend the victim from Kevin's verbal attacks made me realize how much I hated myself for compromising my values and becoming someone I never wanted to be. In that moment, I knew I wanted to be like Tony, to stand up for what was right and not just follow the crowd for the sake of fitting in. It wasn't an instantaneous change, but it was a turning point that made me understand the importance of being true to my own values and beliefs rather than seeking safety in the herd.

Now, let's consider another scenario. Imagine you have made a conscious decision to avoid alcohol due to the negative health effects experienced by your father. One night, while out with friends, they insist on ordering drinks and pressure you into joining them. Deep down, you know you should stick to your principles, but the fear of being excluded or judged as the odd one out weighs heavily on your mind. In the end, you give in and have a drink just to appease your friends. In this situation, your own wishes and values were thrown out the window due to peer pressure - a common occurrence in our lives.

Often, we only realize that our chosen path is not the one we truly wanted much later on. And by then, you may feel it's too late to change course. But there is a valuable lesson we can all learn: marching to the beat of our own drum is a perfectly valid option. Yes, it may not be the easiest road to take, as it can leave us feeling isolated and different from the herd. It takes courage to break away from societal norms and expectations.

But being true to ourselves and living authentically can also attract like-minded individuals into our lives. Those who share similar thoughts and behaviors. Despite the potential for loneliness and uncertainty, remember that it's always worth waiting for the right people and groups that align with your dreams, values, and current state of being.

It's important to remember that you cannot blindly follow the wishes of others. You must use your own brain to think for yourself. Tune out the outside noise and start living your own life. Don't let others' opinions dictate your actions or limit your potential. Follow your own heart and stay true to yourself, even if it means going against the crowd.

In the first lesson, we discussed the potential gains of stepping outside your comfort zone. It's a leap that requires energy and some risk, but the rewards can be significant. However, sometimes people take this leap toward something they don't truly desire. They may be so invested in following the crowd that they blindly step into a situation that doesn't align with their own goals or values.

This approach can be counterproductive. If you're going to take a risk, make it meaningful. Choose something that excites YOU, aligns with YOUR passions, and helps you grow as an individual. Remember, it's your comfort zone, and ultimately, it's your choice.

Remember.

This is your life.

This is YOUR story.

16.

BE YOURSELF WITH YOUR PARTNER

Authenticity is key in any relationship. Many people try to put on a façade, hiding their true selves to attract a potential partner. But the truth is, pretending to be someone you're not is exhausting and can lead to an unhealthy dynamic. This lesson may seem simple, but it's one that I had to learn the hard way - just be yourself with your partner.

Don't try to hide your true feelings or pretend to like something that you actually hate just to please your significant other. Open communication and honesty are crucial for a healthy and lasting relationship. Of course, compromise and sacrifices are necessary at times, but it's important to maintain transparency and authenticity.

I've seen many couples who were incompatible from the start but stayed together for months or even years before realizing they weren't right for each other. Often, this is because one or both partners were playing an act that wasn't truly them to keep the relationship going. But shouldn't a relationship be a place where you are accepted and loved for who you truly are?

For a long time, I was guilty of being a chameleon in relationships. I would change my behavior to impress someone I liked. But it never worked for me. In fact, one relationship was so draining that driving towards my ex-girlfriend's place felt like going to the gym at 5 in the morning (and for me that is crazy hard!). That's when I decided to give up on love and dating altogether. I also gave up the mask. Then, by simply being my silly, film-loving, dream-chasing self, I landed a date with Maria - who is now my wife and mother of our two beautiful children.

Being yourself doesn't mean being complacent or not striving to improve as a person. It simply means embracing your true self and feeling comfortable enough with your partner to let your guard down. Remember, it's better to be single than in a relationship where you cannot be yourself. So don't be afraid to let your true colors shine in a relationship, because that's when you'll truly find happiness and compatibility.

17.

TRY NOT TO KILL YOURSELF

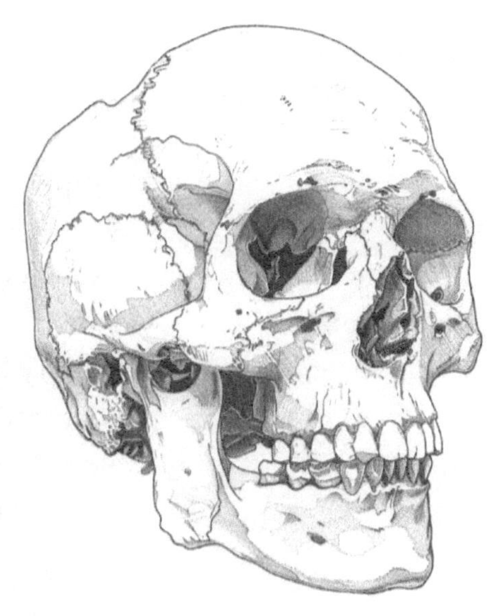

"Oh come on man. Isn't this obvious?" you may ask.

Well.. if it's that obvious then why are we trying to kill ourselves everyday?

"Am I?" you might reply.

Numbers incoming. The World Health Organization estimates that over 8 million deaths a year are due to tobacco use alone. Worldwide, 3 million people die from alcohol-related causes annually.

Well, let's bring up some of the common ways we are killing ourselves in our daily lives:

- The heavy weight of alcohol on our livers and hearts.
- The adrenaline rush as we speed down highways.
- The greasy comfort of processed and fast food.
- The lack of movement in our sedentary lives.
- The avoidance of seeking help when pain creeps in or when we face mental distress.
- The constant pull of a cigarette between our fingers.
- The overwhelming stress of work.
- The toxic grip of abusive relationships or workplaces.

These are just some examples. We all know deep down how destructive these habits can be, yet we continue to indulge in them. It's so much easier to ignore the consequences and keep living in the moment.

Double Big Mac with Bacon? Sure. Pint of Coke? Definitely. Tequila shots? Woohoo! Another round? Sweet! Drive home or get a cab? Drive, for sure. Hey, bro, slow down, it's a 60 (km/h) zone. Nah... feel the need for speed!

The truth is, we are making some choices that are slowly killing us.

I know this firsthand. My liver isn't in stellar condition and my blood count values have been far from ideal for years now. I blame a multitude of factors: an unhealthy diet filled with fast food, lack of physical activity, sitting all day long, and my love for alcohol - particularly all those thousands of Negronis I've consumed over the decades. And let's not forget about the stress.

So what should I do now?

Should I give up and spiral into an early grave? Or should I make an effort to turn things around? The answer is clear - I want to live a longer, healthier and more meaningful life.

Do I know what I need to do? Sometimes it's obvious, like cutting back on alcohol. Other times, it's more complex, like figuring out how to be less stressed at work. There are a few questions to consider: Can you talk to your boss about your workload? Could you prioritize tasks differently or manage your time better? Is it possible that this job just isn't the right fit for you?

Whichever path you choose to take, it's very hard.

Yes, it's incredibly difficult.

If you're struggling with unhealthy habits or behaviors, please seek help. Talk to a doctor, therapist, or trusted friend. You can maybe start with a friend. Your friend might not be an expert on the topic but sharing your struggles with at least one other person might take a lot of weight off your chest. Also there are tons of resources online available to support you on your journey to a healthier and happier life.

Don't be discouraged if you want to change but find it difficult. Setbacks are normal, but they don't define you. You're moving forward, and that's what matters. One small step back is nothing compared to the journey you're on. Losing weight is not something that just happens in a week. It will take months and it's about healthy habits and discipline. I know it's easier said than done and my beer belly is nodding as I'm writing this.

And do surround yourself with people who have healthier habits. Being around those who are drunk all the time can make sobriety a hell more challenging.

Remember, it's worth it. After all, we only have one life.

One precious, fleeting chance to make the most of our time on this Earth.

18.

FRIENDS COME AND FRIENDS GO

Friendships are a voyage filled with hellos and goodbyes, much like the rise and fall of ocean waves. As we mature, we acknowledge that some friendships only last for a certain time or stage in our lives, while others may withstand the test of time. When we were young, we often held onto the idea that all close friendships would never end, but as we gain experience, we learn that this is not always true.

I have changed jobs five times in my life, and with each new workplace came the opportunity to meet new people and form new friendships. Some of these individuals became close friends, but as I moved on to new opportunities, our ties inevitably loosened. The familiar words "Let's keep in touch" were often exchanged, but as days turned into months and months turned into years, those once-close friendships faded into distant memories. There is a saying in Maltese that goes "Il-boghod mill-ghajn, il-boghod mill-qalb" - far from the eyes, far from the heart. It aptly describes how distance can weaken even the strongest bonds between friends.

In today's fast-paced world where time is a precious commodity, it can be challenging to maintain constant contact with all of our past and present friends. Despite technological advancements such as the internet and social media, virtual connections cannot replace the value of face-to-face interactions and shared experiences. The term "friends" on social media has taken on a different meaning than what true friendship entails.

While accepting that not all friendships will stand the test of time may be a bitter pill to swallow, it is not all doom and gloom. Some friendships do stand the test of time; I have been close friends with my friend Bernard since 1995. And wherever life takes us, we will continue to make new friends who will join us in sharing our current chapter in life.

The lesson here is to cherish and make the most out of our friendships, knowing that not all of them will last. But those that do are precious treasures that enrich our lives in ways we could have never imagined.

19.

PAUSE. THINK. THRIVE.

Close your eyes and take a deep breath in through your nose, filling your lungs with the clean air around you (don't do this in the middle of a city street). Hold it for a moment, letting the oxygen seep through your body and calm your mind. Now slowly exhale, releasing any tension or stress you may have been holding onto.

As you sit here in this quiet moment, think back on the past week of your life. How did you spend your time? Work, household chores, caring for loved ones, errands and appointments, social outings and digital distractions all likely filled your days. Perhaps there was even some unexpected drama or conflict that added to the chaos.

But in the midst of this busy cycle called life, did you ever truly pause?

Not just taking a break to grab coffee, eat a Kit Kat or scroll through social media, but a real pause where you step back from it all and simply be still. We all need a moment to catch our breath from this marathon and reflect on ourselves and our situation.

Some call meditation some 'new-age shit'. This 'shit' has been around for thousands of years and is scientifically proven to reduce stress and anxiety and promote focus and our health. Suffering from stress and lack of focus?

Might as well give it a shot! It's free and takes a few moments.

One thing that I really really hate is people bragging about how busy they are. They constantly jump from one thing to another, packing their days so full there's no time for lunch, let alone a moment to breathe. They brag about their endless cups of coffee, as if constant busyness is a badge of honor.

The problem? By the end of the day, they're so exhausted they can't think straight, reflect, or even relax. This constant pressure leads to impulsive decisions, burnout, and a plethora of missed learning opportunities. Worst of all, they lose sight of what truly matters in life.

So please, join me now in this pause.

Find a quiet space without distractions, where you can open up and be honest with yourself. What should you do next?

Ask yourself these questions and answer them truthfully:

- How am I feeling lately?
- What am I grateful for?
- What have I learned recently?
- What have I accomplished lately?
- What is important for me to focus on next?

As you take this time to reflect, you may discover new insights about yourself and your priorities. This small pause will help you regain perspective and control over your life. Don't just exist and rush from one task to the next - take breaks and reflect.

This book itself is the product of many pauses like this. The lessons within are the result of my own reflections on experiences I have had. I have listed my lessons, but remember that each person's journey is unique, so pay attention to your own lessons as well.

You'll soon realize that history often repeats itself, and with a wiser mind from these pauses, you'll be better equipped to handle whatever life throws your way.

Remember to pause.

You'll get back from your pause a wiser person.

20.

CHANGE IS CONSTANT. EMBRACE THE RIDE.

Be prepared for change, whether it is welcome or not.

As the wise Greek philosopher Heraclitus once said, "Change is the only constant." It will occur sooner or later, without our control. And while we may not always have a say in these changes, we can certainly influence them, as previously mentioned in another lesson.

Here are just a few examples of inevitable changes in life:

- The Actions of others

- Aging and all its effects

- Our society, its ideals and culture

- Evolving or disappearing relationships

- Residential and environmental transformations

- Interactions and decisions that shape our path

- And finally the ultimate change - death

These are all part of the human experience. Life is dynamic and we will face countless changes throughout our journey. It could be a new boss at work, a relocation to a different neighborhood, a sudden tax increase imposed by the government, or even something as small as your hairline starting to recede or an unexpected storm on a Sunday. There will also be new people entering our lives and old ones leaving, accidents happening, sickness striking, conflicts arising, and the weather constantly changing. The list goes on. Also COVID happened in 2020 - who was expecting that one?

My point is this: We must accept that change is an inevitable part of life and that most of it is out of our control. Even those rare moments when everything seems perfect - your health, your job, your relationship - will eventually come to an end. On the other hand, those times when everything feels like it's falling apart - when nothing makes sense and you just want to cry - will also pass. Why? Because change happens. Time moves forward.

I fondly remember hopping on board my grandpa's old Land Rover during my childhood, piled in with my family, aunts, uncles, and cousins, as we headed to the sister island of Gozo for a fun day on the island. I'm not sure if it was ever legal to fit so many people in one car! Exploring this new world (for me) with my aunts and cousins brought me pure joy. Of course, much has changed since. Grandpa passed away, and later, Grandma too. The Land Rover was likely scrapped. I cherish the few memories I hold onto from that special time.

A wise disco guy once said, "We should party while there's music." We know that eventually the music will stop or the DJ will play a song we hate. So let's dance in this moment and then gracefully face whatever changes come our way. Let's cherish the good times and find strength in facing the challenges that accompany change. This should be our mindset.

We know for a fact that life will throw us many curveballs. What should we do? Adapt. Embrace the challenge. Face uncertainty with a positive attitude. It could be an opportunity for growth and improvement, or a change for the better. No matter what it may bring, let's approach change with an open mind and a willingness to learn and evolve.

It's the best thing we can do.

21.

THE WORLD IS A MASTERPIECE

Have you ever had the opportunity to watch the brilliant TV series Cosmos? This science documentary, originally presented by the brilliant mind of Carl Sagan and, later on, Neil deGrasse Tyson, explores the vastness and complexity of our universe and everything within it.

As I watched this series, and other documentaries about our world and solar system, I couldn't help but feel overwhelmed and humbled by the immensity and unfathomable beauty of our universe.

Consider this - our universe is 13.7 billion years old. Earth and our moon were formed 4.5 billion years ago. Life on Earth began 3.7 billion years ago in the depths of our oceans. Modern humans evolved a mere 200,000 years ago. And now, here you are, reading these words and existing in this moment.

On our planet alone, there are an astonishing 380,000 known species of plants and 1.2 million known species of animals - each one unique and essential to the delicate balance of life on Earth. It is estimated that over 117 billion humans have lived throughout history, with over 8 billion currently living on this vibrant planet we call home.

Take a moment to let those numbers sink in. Our minds struggle to comprehend such vastness and wonder.

I remember a defining moment when I was 18. I had just had my first surgery and was being driven home from the hospital by my parents. As we made our way through the streets, I looked out at the world around me - towering trees, warm sun, fields bursting with plants and flowers, bustling people going about their day, stray cats searching for food- and suddenly realized the magnificence of life all around me. In that moment, any complaints or discomfort from my surgery melted away as I fully appreciated the precious gift that is life.

And this is just the surface. We don't have to look far to see the incredible beauty and complexity of our world - we need only look within ourselves. Our bodies, intricate and efficient machines, capable of breathing, pumping blood, self-healing, and so much more with minimal effort on our part. All it requires is nourishment and care, and it can sustain us for many decades, even over a century.

The next time you find yourself caught up in the chaos of everyday life, take a moment to pause and appreciate the masterpiece that is our universe - from the vast expanse of stars and galaxies to the intricacies of our own bodies. And remember, you are a part of this magnificent tapestry, a living and breathing miracle in the grand scheme of things.

In this vast world, there are people who radiate goodness and kindness. In each of our lives, we have been blessed with at least one person - if not more - who has loved us unconditionally, cared for us selflessly, and brought joy to our hearts. They were the ones who stood by us through the darkest moments of our lives.

But let's not forget that life is not all sunshine and rainbows. Along with the beauty and goodness, there is also sickness, death, natural disasters, and toxic individuals. It may seem like an unfair trade-off, but such is the balance of life. Just as the Yin Yang symbol depicts, for every positive thing in this world, there exists a negative counterpart. And yet, even amid tragedy and chaos, we can find glimmers of hope and light.

Think about it - when disaster strikes, we often see people coming together to help one another. Amidst the destruction, humanity shines through in acts of bravery and compassion. It is a reminder that even in the face of adversity, there is still goodness to be found.

Of course, this topic is starting to delve into deep philosophical territory. We may never fully understand why good and bad things coexist in this world. But perhaps instead of seeking an answer, we should focus on our perspective and attitude towards life. Let us cherish the good moments and strive to leave a positive mark on this world so that it may continue to shine brighter.

As Marilyn Monroe once said, "Keep your head high, keep your chin up, and most importantly, keep smiling, because life's a beautiful thing and there's so much to smile about."

22.

BE A GOOD PERSON. MOST OF THE TIME.

The line between what is considered good and bad is blurred, subject to personal interpretation. However, regardless of where one draws the line, there is a common understanding of what it means to be a good person. Good persons assist those in need, showing patience, respect, and empathy towards others. They possess good manners, using pleasantries such as "please," "thank you," and "sorry." They wait their turn patiently in queues and share with others without hesitation. Above all, a good person does not intentionally harm anyone. They listen attentively and care deeply about others' well-being.

It's admirable to be a kind-hearted individual.

But should you strive for goodness?

Yes. Being a good person cultivates healthy relationships and connections based on trust and respect. It is difficult to fully trust or respect someone who behaves poorly or disrespects you at the slightest provocation. By embodying goodness, we create an environment of harmony and constructive discussions. In general, people shy away from conflict and prefer the company of those who listen, understand, and respect them. Numerous studies show that being a nice person has positive effects on mental well-being, mood, and overall happiness.

Ultimately, it is crucial that we have good role models who inspire us to become better individuals.

But hold on!

Being a good person does not mean being a doormat or sacrificing your own well-being. There are times when being 'nice' is not the appropriate course of action. The threshold for when to stop being agreeable varies for each person - personally, I find it challenging to show respect towards someone who consistently shows me disrespect, or love someone who harbors hatred towards me, or sacrifice myself for someone who couldn't care less about my feelings.

Furthermore, being a good person is not always rewarded. Sometimes, despite our good intentions, we are met with criticism or even worse - the recognition and promotion go to the bad managers who break the rules while we, the diligent and rule-abiding employees, remain stuck at the same level of the corporate ladder. Or perhaps the arrogant person gets the girl, while we, the shy and respectful ones who would treat her like a queen if given the chance, are left alone. Being a good person does not always cause rewards.

Ultimately, it is crucial to be a good person for one's own sake - for our conscience and mental well-being. Great and positive things stem from kind individuals, creating a ripple effect of virtuous actions.

Therefore, my suggestion is to strive to be a good person - one who embodies empathy, patience, respect, and understanding. It will bring light into your life and relationships, inspire others to do the same, and make the world a more beautiful place to live in. Just remember to stand up for yourself when necessary, especially in the face of injustice.

23.

COLOR YOUR WORLD WITH POSITIVITY

It's all about perspective. Facing any new challenge or experience with a positive mindset can make all the difference.

Often, our initial reaction to change is fear and anxiety. We put up a protective barrier, ready to defend ourselves against any potential harm. While this may get us through the experience, it also prevents us from truly enjoying it and getting the most out of it.

Imagine going on a trip to a remote location with a negative attitude. You might convince yourself that you won't have a good time, that it won't be safe, or that you'd rather be somewhere else. This kind of thinking limits your ability to fully appreciate the experience, explore new opportunities, and learn from new adventures. It can also cause stress for those around you and cause overreacting to minor issues. In the end, you'll either have a terrible experience or , at best, one that falls short of true enjoyment.

Now let's consider the opposite approach. Approaching the trip with a sense of excitement and adventure opens endless possibilities. By looking forward to it and maintaining a positive outlook, you'll already be setting yourself up for success well before the trip even begins. And once you're there, you'll be motivated to make the most of every moment. Sure, there may still be setbacks or challenges along the way, but your positive mindset will help you overcome them quickly and continue to enjoy your time. And at the end of it all, you'll have memories that will last a lifetime.

Of course, despite having a positive mindset, things may not always go perfectly according to plan. But having that inner strength and resilience allows you to push through any obstacles and come out stronger on the other side.

This concept applies to so many different scenarios - starting a new job or receiving a promotion, going on a first date or getting married, moving to a new city or starting at a new school. Anytime we step outside of our comfort zone, we must do so with energy and positivity. This not only helps us cope with the unknown but also reduces the stress and anxiety that often accompanies fear.

Sometimes, however, it can feel utterly impossible to see any positives in a truly awful situation. Imagine having the shittiest of days at work, losing your wallet, fighting with your best half, or missing out on a dream audition or opportunity. How can you be positive in those moments? You might even fantasize about a giant sandworm from Dune erupting and swallowing you whole, or wish for the world to end and take your pain away.

So, what should you do in these cases? First, talk to someone who cares about you and lend you a listening ear. Don't force yourself to find a silver lining right away. Just allow yourself time to process your emotions.

Eventually, with time, you might discover a positive perspective on what happened. Perhaps that awful moment was the push you needed to finally quit your hated job. Maybe it helped you realize your stressful situation is controlling your life and a change is necessary. This phenomenon is truly incredible – sometimes, we need to experience hardship to reach better times. We need to go through a bad relationship to understand what qualities make a good partner. We need a negative experience in a particular job to realize that industry or role isn't a good fit. And sometimes, we experience the loss of someone close to appreciate the preciousness of life and the time we have left.

Personally, I have a wallpaper on my work laptop with the words "It's going to be okay" written on it. While this simple phrase may not completely eliminate my anxiety, it serves as a reminder that no matter what challenges come my way, I will survive and ultimately (and eventually) be okay.

It's all about approaching life with a positive mindset and trusting in your ability to overcome any obstacle that may come your way.

24.

ROOTS IN THE PAST, FUTURE IN HANDS.

As we journey through life, our paths cross with countless individuals, each with their own unique stories and experiences. From losing loved ones at a young age to growing up in impoverished neighborhoods, these past events have left indelible marks on our beings. Some may carry fear from being bullied as children, while others hold a deep sense of empathy for those who have suffered. Our pasts, good and bad, have molded us into the people we are today.

We cannot change what has already happened.

What we can influence is how we move forward... what we do next.

Perhaps you've experienced the heartache of a failed marriage, and it has left its mark on your heart and mind. The thought of starting a new relationship brings fear and hesitation, as you carry the weight of that traumatic experience. But what will you do next? Will you allow yourself to be weighed down by the pain of the past? Or will you rise up, reflect on your lessons learned, and give love another chance?

Of course, it's easy to write these words on paper, but in reality it is incredibly difficult. However, it's important to understand that you should not let your past limit your potential for today.

In my 10 years of leadership experience, one of my key responsibilities is helping my team members learn and develop as engineers. I've noticed that much of the constructive feedback I provide during our sessions isn't entirely new to them. People already know what they need to do to grow but they resist growth. Why? There are many reasons why someone might resist growth, and one of the most challenging to address is when an individual has already tried and failed. I remember one team member who reported to me and he excelled at working independently and avoided collaboration like the plague. My initial assumption was that this was due to introversion. However, once I gained his trust, he revealed a past negative experience with a specific colleague, leading him to generalize and avoid all kinds of teamwork. He truly believed he was just bad at working with people.

It's striking how ONE bad experience with one or two people can lead us to create blanket rules that affect all interactions. Do you have a similar experience?

In this case, we agreed that for him to grow he had to join another team and start afresh. This triggered a remarkable change. He thrived in the new environment which was much more welcoming, embraced collaboration, and consistently excelled when working alongside others. He was also happier and fulfilled.

The past mattered little.

When you wake up in the morning, take a moment to sit on your bed as the sunlight pours through your window. Look at your hands and gently clasp them together. These are the very hands that hold the power to shape your present and future. You have been given a fresh canvas of 24 hours. Yes, the past 24 hours, 24 days, 24 years may not have gone according to plan and may have changed you in some way. But today is a new opportunity - how will you paint this day? Will you continue using the dark shades from before, or will you add a pop of color to your canvas today?

Don't give up yet.

Let the present be the defining moment that shapes who you truly want to be.

25.

NO FISHING = NO FISH

This simple equation holds a powerful truth. It serves as a reminder that without effort, there can be no results. Without taking action and risks, there can be no success or achievement.

Let's see your past achievements. Each one was the result of your hard work, determination, and willingness to take a chance. You earned your college degree through countless hours of studying and dedication. You won over the girl of your dreams by improving yourself and taking a leap of faith. You reached the podium in a race because you trained relentlessly for it. You were able to buy your own home after years of working tirelessly to earn enough money. You finished writing your book after pouring endless hours into it. And you have raised a beautiful family because you made sacrifices and invested time and love into them.

Of course, there may be rare instances where luck plays a role in achieving something without much effort on our part. Perhaps winning the lottery or receiving an unexpected inheritance. But for the majority of our goals and dreams, hard work and perseverance are necessary ingredients for success. And that is perfectly okay because the end result is worth it.

For me, my ultimate goal has always been to become a filmmaker. I am a passionate movie lover with many stories to tell and share through film. But simply daydreaming about it while lounging on my sofa did not bring me any closer to realizing this dream. So, I took action by reading books and articles on filmmaking, purchasing a cheap camera, and practicing filming with my brother playing soccer on my mom's rooftop (while trying not to get caught by our neighbors). The end result may have been far from perfect, but it motivated me to pursue this hobby. Years later and several short films later, I received my first filmmaking award for "Best Local Director" in a televised short film festival, and I am grateful for the day I decided to stop daydreaming and start taking action towards my dream.

Just like fishing, there may be days where we don't catch anything despite our efforts. But the key is to remember there are more fish in the sea than on our sofas. So, what is your "fish"? What is your ultimate goal or dream? What do you want to achieve?

It's time to start fishing and make it a reality.

26.

IF YOU'RE NOT HAPPY, DO SOMETHING ABOUT IT

If you find yourself in a state of unhappiness, it's time to act. You have to do something about it. I know, I know - this lesson may seem simple on paper, but when applied to real life, things become much more complicated.

Perhaps your job leaves you feeling drained and unfulfilled. Or maybe your relationship is draining all your energy. You chose the wrong course in school, and now your life feels like a mess. You feel bored or useless. You hate your current situation. And suddenly a choir of voices surrounds you and they sing "Do something about it!" But instead of taking action, you reply with a million excuses. That infamous "but..". And so, nothing changes, and you remain stuck in an unhappy situation. For a long time. Maybe forever.

Sure, some excuses may be valid. For instance, leaving your job may not be an option because of financial commitments like mortgages or debt. Or perhaps staying in the country is necessary because your spouse just landed a great job locally. These are legitimate restrictions and boundaries that can make change seem impossible. However, I urge you to think deeper. If you search hard enough, there is always a way out or a solution that fits within any boundaries.

My suggestion is to set aside your sadness and anger for a moment. Instead, focus on understanding your options and writing them. The potential solutions. Evaluate each one carefully and write down the potential benefits that could come from each option. Don't dwell on potential risks - you already know those. I want you to only focus on the positive outcomes as those are often forgotten when making decisions. Look for an option that has the potential to make you happier with minimal risk, and then start taking small steps in that direction. Remember, there is always a way out if you are willing to find it and take the leap.

I know this story too well. I was once in a job that I absolutely despised. Some of my colleagues were toxic. One time HR even complained about me walking too slowly in the corridor as I'm heading to my desk! I hated being called in to work on Saturdays, dealing with a disorganized company, and struggling to find parking every morning. When I would complain about my job at home, my wife would always tell me to start looking for other opportunities. But for a while, I made excuses not to leave. "It's getting better" (it wasn't - I was just getting used to the misery) or "All workplaces are like this." Finally, I mustered up the courage to start applying for other jobs, and I landed a position at a new company that was a hundred times better than my previous one. So no, not all jobs are miserable and draining like my old one.

Remember this: no one is coming to save you.

We often find ourselves clinging to a familiar situation, even if it's bringing us down. We find ourselves on a sinking boat. This "boat" could be a bad job, a toxic relationship, or a difficult period in life. We stay put, looking for a miracle through the porthole, waiting for someone to rescue us or for a magical opportunity to appear. Screaming "Superman! Help me!" does nothing. Time passes, and nothing changes. We watch our life slowly slip away.

The key? Take action.

Happiness doesn't come knocking. It's worth taking the risk to pursue it. You deserve happiness, and you deserve to take steps towards creating a more fulfilling life for yourself.

27.

WORK BUT DON'T SLAVE TO IT.

Money. It's the essential fuel that keeps us moving forward in life, powering our ability to survive and enjoy its many offerings. With money, we can purchase food and drinks, pay our bills and hairdresser, hail a taxi or book a flight, splurge on new clothes or furnish our homes, indulge in a vacation or treat ourselves to a massage - the possibilities are endless. Money is not just a means of survival, it's also a symbol of success, comfort, and power.

But earning money requires work. Work can take many forms - from providing a service or creating a product for someone else to paying for goods and services offered by others. In essence, jobs are the backbone of modern society, allowing us to exchange skills and resources for monetary compensation. Without an income channel, life becomes exponentially harder, making it super important to excel in our chosen field to thrive.

To achieve excellence at work, we must constantly strive to learn and improve our skills, becoming more valuable and trustworthy as employees. This can lead to recognition, promotions, or salary increases. The same principle applies for entrepreneurs running their own businesses - they must work hard to keep their company afloat and profitable. Focus and drive at work are crucial for success.

However, it's important not to let work consume us entirely.

On our deathbeds, we won't be proud of the extra hours spent at the office or the countless business targets achieved. In my 20 years in the workforce, I've encountered individuals who were consumed by their ambition to climb the corporate ladder. They sacrificed precious time with loved ones and neglected simple joys in life along the way. Their obsession with hitting business targets often resulted in arrogant treatment towards those reporting to them. In the end, they lost their souls. Sure, they may have earned more money but was it worth missing out on precious moments with their children or partner? Even their mental health suffered as they navigated through constant high-stress situations with shareholders or upper management breathing down their necks. While some stress can push us to do more and challenge our limits, constant and excessive stress can be detrimental to our well-being, especially mental health.

During my time as a software developer, I honed my skills and gained the trust of my superiors, leading to more responsibilities and new titles. I was determined to prove myself and worked tirelessly on two major projects, often putting in long hours. I also took on roles in team leadership, pushing me out of my comfort zone. I was on fire and content until two events changed everything. One event was a failure, while the other became one of the most cherished moments in my life.

The failure was as a project at work that was poorly conceived, planned and executed, resulting in chaos, stress and disappointment. In those dark days, I felt an overwhelming sense of drama and constant stress, teetering on the verge of tears. Though no one directly accused me of any wrongdoing, everyone felt like we messed this one up despite our best efforts. I couldn't help but feel that all the previous successes my teams and I had achieved were rendered insignificant in light of this failure. In time, this made me realize that what truly matters is personal growth and experience - for ultimately, people forget the successes you were part of and move on from any of your past achievements.

The second event that altered my life was the birth of my first daughter, Julie. Marriage itself did not bring me about any significant changes, but when Julie entered the world, everything changed drastically. It forced me to pause, reflect, and reassess my priorities. While work and money are undeniably important aspects of life, there are greater things to value: family and loved ones, meaningful experiences and connections, physical and mental well-being, passions, and time.

This realization did not diminish my dedication or effort towards my job. Rather, it taught me to view work as a means to make a living and develop skills. After work hours, I learned to shift my focus to what truly matters: nurturing relationships with family and friends, enjoying life's experiences, pursuing passions, and taking care of myself.

28.

LEARN TO SAY NO

"Can you lend a hand with my project?" Her voice was pleading, and you knew that saying yes would mean sacrificing your own precious time and focus on your own work. But being the nice guy you are, you agree to help. Then you had to rush your own project. I was guilty of this.

"Are you joining us at the party tonight? Everyone will be there." You've never really enjoyed those types of parties, but you don't want to seem like a loner or outcast, so you reluctantly say yes. You got here. You don't enjoy it but at least you don't look like a loser. I was guilty of this.

Drowning in work, your heart stops as your boss approaches with another "small thing" to finish by day's end. "I'm super busy, but… I'll try to manage it," you say, forcing a smile. You know this likely means missing dinner with the kids and you'll miss all the stories they wanted to share with you before going to sleep, but you can't bear to disappoint your boss. I was guilty of this.

We've all been there before - saying yes when we should have said no. Saying "of course" when "sorry, no" is what we wanted to say.

But why is it so hard to say no?

Often, it's because we fear disappointing others or getting into conflicts. We feel obligated to say yes to avoid feeling guilty or rejected. We don't want to feel the discomfort that comes with refusal.

But here's the thing: it's super important to learn to say no more often. While there may be times where sacrifices are necessary for the ones we love and care for, it's crucial to prioritize our own needs and wants too. We need to be honest with ourselves and not follow the crowd just for the sake of fitting in. We need to prioritize our time and not let others take care of prioritizing our lives.

By being true to yourself and learning to decline things that don't align with your priorities and vision, you'll gain a sense of control over your life and future. You'll also have more time and energy to dedicate towards your passions. And as a bonus, you'll attract people who respect your decisions and support your path.

29.

SOCIAL MEDIA IS A BEAST

Have you ever realized how sometimes what you read on social media can affect you emotionally? Let me give you a recent example.

I was in a Facebook group for people who share and discuss a certain specific topic (let's say music). There's one member who frequently posts hateful or controversial statements. For instance, he might say, "Moby's latest song is shit. So boring and uninspiring. He's lost his touch, and his fans just get excited by any crap he releases."

Then there's me, fuming after reading it. I clench my fists, hover my fingers atop the keyboard and type a scathing reply like "STFU" or "You have no taste" or I try to justify the merit of the song to provide a counter argument. I know that if I reply, it will lead to an endless, pointless argument. I'd be angry and frustrated over something insignificant. It wouldn't matter in the long run. It wouldn't even matter now. His post, my post - changes nothing. I would waste time and energy better spent elsewhere.

For this and many similar reasons, I ended up leaving the group and also reduced my social media usage. I still check Facebook occasionally for updates like births and marriages.

My experience is just a small example, but many people experience emotional turmoil due to seemingly minor social media interactions – a photo, a comment, a reaction, a message. Cyberbullying is a reality, and so is comparing yourself to the seemingly perfect lives others curate online. The need for constant approval can also be a major source of unhappiness.

This isn't surprising when you consider the vast reach of social media. As of January 2024, according to Datareportal research, a staggering 62% of the world, or 5 billion people, use social media daily. With an average daily usage of 2 hours and 23 minutes, that's a significant amount of time spent in a potentially emotionally charged environment.

Social media isn't inherently bad. It can connect us to loved ones, expose us to diverse viewpoints, and foster a sense of belonging. However, countless studies highlight the link between excessive social media use and increased anxiety, depression, and insomnia.

Exclusion in the age of social media takes a new form. In the 90s, being left out of a party meant feeling sad. Today, you see pictures and videos plastered online, amplifying the feeling of isolation. This curated portrayal of 'fun' can be particularly damaging.

Here are some tips from my own experience on how I learned to handle social media so that it doesn't make me sad and depressed:

- Unfriend, unfollow, leave anything or anyone that is making you feel sad, angry or any other negative emotions. They are not worth your time.

- Seek out people that inspire you, motivate you, teach you or entertain you.

- Remember you are different. Don't compare yourself to others. Others are definitely sharing the best things that happened to them, and omitting all the bad things happening. Just be yourself. Who likes you may follow you. This is your journey.

- Stay in touch with people that care about you. Share and spread joy.

- Don't spend too much time on it. Use your time wisely. Remember that most of the time you are getting nothing out of it. Remember your goals!

30.

BE OPEN TO CRITICISM. YOU ARE FAR FROM PERFECT.

At the young age of 19, I took on the ambitious task of filming my first scripted short film. My love for superheroes inspired me to create "Justice Kid," a story about a boy in a rural village who believes he has superpowers but in reality, has none. Despite this, he consistently defeats the villains through sheer determination. Filming during my summer break from university, I poured my heart and soul into this project and was bursting with pride when it was complete. In fact, I was so proud that I created dozens of DVDs of this 15 minute short film and eagerly handed them out to my classmates when school resumed.

But then came the feedback. Some of my closest friends praised it, while others didn't even bother watching it. Some did not particularly like it and there were those who gave me brutally honest criticism. One person in particular delivered a lengthy speech about why he thought my film was lacking. Instantly, I felt a surge of anger towards him and couldn't understand how he could be so harsh. Didn't he know how much time and effort I put into this? How dare he call it anything less than amazing?

However, after a few months passed, I gathered up the courage to rewatch my short film. And as much as it pained me to admit, that person was right. It did have lots of flaws and shortcomings that I had failed to see before. Choppy editing, flawed filming, horrendous sound. Maybe "sucks" was too strong of a word, but it definitely was way far from perfect.

Through this experience, and many others in life, I learned that we often become defensive when someone criticizes something we hold dear. We only want to hear praise and disregard any negative feedback because it's uncomfortable and can bruise our egos. But in doing so, we miss opportunities for growth.

It is important to listen and reflect on feedback before responding defensively. Ask yourself, "Could they be right?" or "Is there something I can learn from this?" Remember that opinions and preferences are subjective. Just because someone doesn't like something, it doesn't mean it's inherently bad. It could simply mean they have different expectations or perspectives. And ultimately, who is to say what is perfect? What may be close to perfect to one person may be considered mediocre by another.

I've also learned to apply this mindset in other aspects of my life. For instance, when I spend hours working on a household project and proudly present it to my wife, her initial reaction may not always be positive. Instead of getting defensive and telling her to do it herself if she thinks she can do better, I take a step back and evaluate her feedback. If she's right, I make the necessary changes.

Here we have tips I found helpful when handling criticism:

- Remain calm and avoid reacting impulsively.

- Ask for clarification if needed.

- Reflect what you can learn from the feedback.

- Don't take it personally; it's about the work, not your worth as a person.

- Filter comments you feel are unfair. Hate has many forms. Envy can be very harmful. Assholes are everywhere.

- Use criticism as a growth opportunity and move on.

31.

EMPATHY IS GOLD. CHARITY IS DIAMOND.

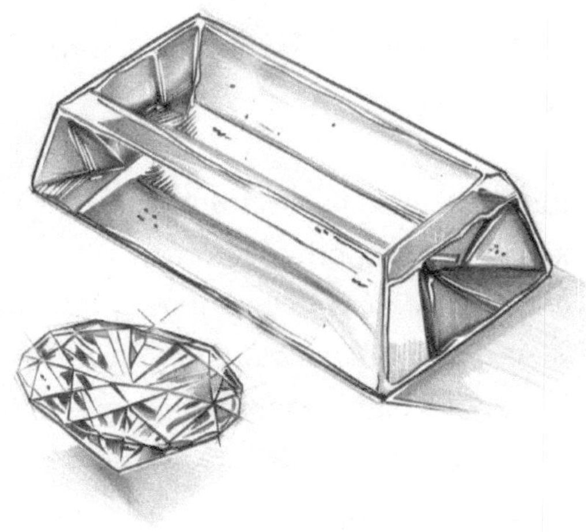

Empathy is a precious and valuable ability, shining like gold in a world that can often be hardened and cold (it rhymes!). It allows us to connect on a deeper level with others, understanding and caring for their feelings. Without empathy, we would simply be self-interested beings coexisting without any true connection.

If you truly try to understand others, listen to them carefully and try to put yourself in their shoes, you will build stronger relationships built on trust and compassion. The more you understand others, the more likely you would help them, have more meaningful connections and ultimately make your group/family/community a better place. Empathy is like the glue that binds people.

But unfortunately, in some environments, empathy is pushed aside in favor of other priorities. I have experienced this firsthand in one of my previous workplaces. When someone suddenly begins underperforming, a bad leader may jump to harsh criticism instead of taking the time to understand what may be causing the change in output. A good leader, on the other hand, would ask questions and offer support, recognizing that there may be personal struggles or hardships affecting the individual's performance. Sadly, I encountered more bad leaders than good in my time.

And then there's "Charity is Diamond". When empathy turns into action, it becomes charity - a rare and precious gift that shines like diamonds. Charity takes many forms: giving money, donating goods, donating blood, sharing knowledge, or volunteering time. It is about selflessly helping those in need without expecting anything in return. And it is truly beautiful. Not only does it bring joy and comfort to the recipient, but it also brings happiness and fulfillment to the giver. Like diamonds, charity has the power to leave a lasting impact on so many people.

I consider charity an effort to make the world a bit more fair than it currently is. It's about restoring a bit of balance. It's about making a positive difference in an unfair world where some are suffering more than others. Knowing you are making a positive impact can be a great motivator to your sense of purpose. It can make you happier and increase your self-worth.

'L-Istrina' is a 12-hour Maltese TV program that lets viewers call in with donations to Malta's Community Chest Fund - a charitable organization. Heartbreaking video clips telling stories of people battling illnesses (some of which are very rare), disabilities, and accidents unfold during the show. You hear the stories of so many people and children that have gone through hell while still on Earth. These stories make me realize that there are so many people out there, millions of people, that are suffering at this very moment, while we are reading this book and sipping our coffee. I'm always blown away by so many amazing people that utilize their limited time on Earth to help those in need. Isn't it beautiful? So how can we help? The least we could do is share a little bit of what we have - even a small donation can make a big difference in someone's life. Do research reputable charities and do consider helping them. Trust me, you'll feel great knowing you made a positive impact. You could make an online donation right now.

How does it feel?

Together, empathy and charity add a little bit more meaning and purpose to our lives, bringing light and goodness to the world around us.

I have to finish this lesson by sharing one of my favorite non-profit charity organizations. It is special because it puts 100% of public donations directly to fund clean water projects around the world. The charity is called Charity Water and you can find more by visiting www.charitywater.org.

32.

MAKE USE OF POWERFUL WORDS

The weight of our words cannot be underestimated. Each word we speak has the power to evoke strong emotions and create lasting impacts on those who receive them. Think about words like 'thank you', 'I love you', 'I appreciate your effort', 'you look beautiful', 'I'm sorry', 'I believe in you', 'this is amazing', and countless others.

How often do we use these words? And when we do, do we truly mean them?

These simple yet powerful words have the ability to make someone's day or completely shatter their confidence. Imagine your partner spends all day preparing a special dinner for you. If it turns out to be delicious, the least you can do is say "Thank you. That was incredible!" This shows appreciation for their effort and encourages them to continue trying new things. But let's say the dinner is a disaster - burnt, overcooked, or just plain terrible. If Gordon Ramsey was there he would have thrown the plate out of the window. How would you react? Saying "This is bad! So you spent a whole day cooking this? Let's just order takeout." not only crushes their spirits but also discourages them from ever trying again. Instead, consider saying something like "It may not have turned out as expected, but I appreciate all the hard work you put into this. I know next time it will be better." This shows understanding and support, and might even motivate them to learn from their mistakes and try again.

And then, of course, there is no denying the impact of the three little words: 'I love you'. As a child, my mother constantly told me to say "I love you" to her, and I would always respond with the same words. But as I grew into a teenager, I found myself saying it less and less, perhaps because I thought showing emotions was a sign of weakness for a man. However, after many years and becoming a parent myself, I realized the true depth of love and sacrifice that comes with raising children. Now when my kids spontaneously tell me "I love you," it fills me with joy. And thanks to them, I have also started telling my mother "I love you" again, just like in my childhood days.

Take a moment to think about the people in your life who deserve more appreciation, attention and love than you have shown. It could be your partner, parents, siblings, children, friends, colleagues, or even your neighbors. Who deserves an apology from you? Who deserves to hear "I'm sorry" even if it may not fix everything? Who would appreciate hearing "Thank you for being my friend" even if you have never told them before? Is there someone in your life with a dream or struggle who could use some encouragement with an "I believe in you"?

Our words hold immense power. They can either bring others down or lift them up. They can change the course of someone's life. They may ruin someone's day or bring a smile that carries them through it. But the most important thing is that we truly mean what we say.

And finally... Thank you for choosing to read my book :)

33.

MONEY DOES NOT BRING HAPPINESS BUT EASES THE WAY

While money can't buy happiness, it can provide comfort and a range of options. It is often seen as a necessary evil, capable of both good and bad deeds. On one hand, it allows for basic needs to be met and luxuries to be enjoyed, while on the other, it can fuel greed, corruption, and materialism. In fact, many negative world events are often centered around money.

But despite its flaws, we cannot deny the importance of money in our lives. It allows us to survive and indulge in pleasures that make life more comfortable and interesting. It opens up doors for travel, education, investments, and better healthcare. So while some may argue that money doesn't bring happiness, it certainly brings plenty of benefits.

You may say to me, "Please don't spout the 'money doesn't bring happiness' bullshit. Money does make me happy." And you wouldn't be wrong… to an extent. Having enough money to cover expenses and live in a decent environment does bring happiness. But beyond a certain point lies diminishing returns. Once your needs are met, each extra Euro or Dollar will bring you less joy than the previous one. Pursuing more money can lead to a never-ending chase where obsession takes over and sacrifices are made to attain wealth.

Ironically, the more money you have, the more you often want! It's something called the Paradox of Desire. I remember my first promotion at work. I was happy with my first salary increase... for a while. But then I started wanting more! Much more! It was like a hunger I couldn't satisfy. I was always on the hunt for the next raise or some get-rich-quick scheme. (Don't even get me started on the money I lost on crypto. Let's just skip that part.)

It is important to remember that money is merely a tool, not the end goal of happiness. Money does not guarantee happiness. Money does not fill any emotional void.

Ever notice how some people seem obsessed with money? They're constantly thinking: "How can I get rich and quit work?" While financial security is important, remember that this chase shouldn't consume your life. The constant pursuit of wealth can be a major stressor, leading you to neglect your health and relationships. A healthy balance is vital!

Money also has the power to corrupt, turning people into monsters consumed by greed. This can lead to conflicts, scandals, and a loss of morality. We've all heard stories of siblings feuding over inheritances, politicians stealing taxpayer funds, and corporations dodging their fair share of taxes. Some individuals even sacrifice their dignity and self-respect, resorting to selling their bodies for financial gain.

Money is something you should definitely handle responsibly. Spending everything you earn right away shows a lack of control and no thought for the future. I remember the first few years of my career – every paycheck felt like a golden ticket to buy whatever I wanted. I blew it all on stupid shit: video games, PlayStation accessories, endless magazines, t-shirts I never wore, and, of course, alcohol and fast food. What was left barely covered the essentials, and saving was a rare occurrence. Eventually, I got smarter and started saving for a few reasons: emergencies, holidays, and eventually buying my own place. I've found it really helpful to put aside 25% of my salary as soon as I get it and try to live on the remaining 75% for the month. It works for me, even though I still buy stupid shit sometimes.

Nowadays, I find most joy in spending money on experiences, especially traveling or taking on an adventure I've never done before. I do believe that such memories last a long while, and so are a huge investment. I also feel that true joy comes from meaningful relationships, a sense of purpose, personal growth, life experiences and living a fulfilling life.

34.

NEVER STOP LEARNING

As the sun slowly sets behind the horizon, casting a golden glow over the world, I will share with you two of my favorite quotes:

"The only true wisdom is in knowing you know nothing" - Socrates

"Anyone who stops learning is old, whether at 20 or 80. Anyone who keeps learning stays young." - Henry Ford

The words of Socrates remind us that no matter how much knowledge we possess, there will always be an infinity of things left to discover. It is our duty to stay humble and continue to absorb as much as possible throughout our lives, as the visionary Henry Ford wisely pointed out. The pursuit of knowledge and the desire to learn will keep us forever young, sharp, and driven.

But why do so many people give up on learning? Why do they deprioritize it and choose instead to numb their minds with endless brainless entertainment?

Perhaps it's easier to binge-watch Netflix or mindlessly scroll through social media than it is to challenge ourselves and engage in new learning experiences. However, the satisfaction and fulfillment that come from acquiring new skills, expanding our understanding of the world, and nurturing our hobbies are truly enriching and incredible.

Let me share a recent example of how learning opportunities can be found everywhere. We noticed water leaking under the toilet in our main bathroom. It's a "closed coupled toilet" (I had to Google it), meaning the pipes are hidden. I was ready to call a plumber, but my wife suggested we try fixing it ourselves. We knew nothing about toilets, but figured we'd learn something. The plumber can be plan B.

After watching a few YouTube videos, we moved the toilet and discovered the fascinating world underneath. There was a broken pipe and a nearly broken flush mechanism. Once we figured out what was wrong, I dug out my dusty toolbox and got to work. I may have broken something else in the process, but eventually, we fixed the leak and replaced the flush system with a new one.

I learned a lot that day. Sure, calling a plumber would have given me more time to binge-watch TV, but by taking this route, I gained valuable knowledge about how toilets work and how to repair one.

Of course, while we should never stop learning, we must also question everything we learn. In this age of information overload and fake news, it is crucial to research, investigate and seek different perspectives before fully accepting something as truth. Let us not be deceived by flashy headlines or false claims. Instead, let us use our wisdom and critical thinking skills to discern what is genuine and what is not. After all, true learning goes beyond just accepting information at face value – it involves actively engaging with it and using our own judgment to form our beliefs.

There's a universe of knowledge out there. Sciences, Arts, Languages, Business, Philosophy, Technology, Cultures - an endless world of opportunities for growth and discovery.

What do you want to learn?

What will you learn next?

35.

MASTER PATIENCE: THE ROAD IS LONG

Imagine if you could choose a superpower - what would it be? Invisibility, flying, super strength, or healing may come to mind, but I bet "patience" wouldn't be at the top of anyone's list. It's not as flashy or exciting as other abilities, but it is one that we all have the potential to possess.

Patience can be our ultimate weapon against anger, frustration, mistakes, setbacks and endless suffering. It may not seem like much, but it is awesome.

So how do we acquire this superpower?

The ironic thing about developing patience is that it takes time, effort, and of course... patience! I feel like it took me decades to fully understand its power and develop it.

The first step is understanding that great things in life take time. Whether it's a project, skill or dream, success doesn't happen overnight. Just look at sports champions - they dedicated years of training, failures, and learning before achieving greatness. Mastery is a long process that requires dedication and perseverance. And even with relationships and businesses - they require time and effort to grow and thrive.

You cannot give up on your first setbacks! You're not a machine that is designed to do a function and you just switch it on and voila! You're a learning machine that requires experimentation and failure, in order to learn and succeed.

Sure, we sometimes hear stories of overnight success, but what we don't see are the years of preparation and hard work leading up to that moment. So next time you feel yourself becoming impatient with a goal or project, remember that good things take time.

Have you ever felt like running away after a bad day at a new job, project, or relationship? I have, many times. A rough first week at work can make you question your decision to leave your previous job, but that's completely normal. It's important to be patient and give it a few months to see if you fit in.

Sometimes, however, it doesn't work out even after you give it some time, and that's okay. That is what happened to me. In the first week of a particular job everything was going bad - I had to use ancient technology, the workload was overwhelming for the few people we were, and on top of it I struggled to find a parking space every morning. After a few months I started looking for another job. But in other cases, it was worth sticking with.

I'm still at the same job I started 11 years ago, and it's been worth it! The first setback is not an indication of a bad choice. If that was the case, we might as well not do any choice at all as they all come with ups and downs.

There is a Japanese saying which goes like this: "If you feel like you're losing everything, remember that trees lose their leaves every year and they still stand tall and wait for better days to come.". They are patient because bad days are just part of the journey.

I believe patience helped me to be calmer and less stressful. We all know that if we're impatient we would be constantly stressed out, we would rush into decisions, we would be less likely to enjoy the journey and most probably we would make more stupid mistakes. The important thing to remember is patience is all about trusting the process, people, and the power of time.

So my last suggestion is to enjoy the journey and trust in your ability to cultivate this valuable superpower. Because in the end, patience truly is a superpower worth having.

36.

LISTEN

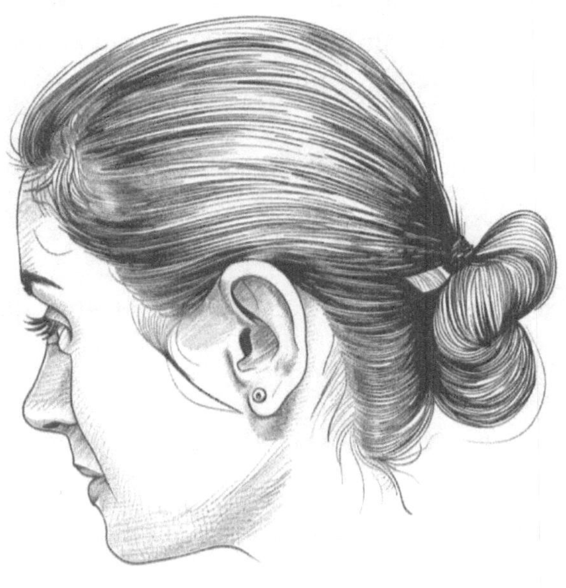

This is another lesson that I wish I had truly understood in my 20s. For so long, my own strong opinions and desire blinded me to always have something to say. When others spoke to me, instead of truly listening and trying to understand their words and feelings, I would already be formulating my response as they are speaking. To me, it seemed more important to share my thoughts than to truly understand the other person. But now I know that most of my past interactions were shallow and lacked true value. If only I had been patient and asked more questions, perhaps things would have been different.

Let me give you an example.

John: I'm not feeling well. Lately, I've been struggling to sleep.

Me: Yeah, same here. Must be the cold weather.

John: Actually, I don't think…

Me: Have you tried wearing warmer clothes before bed? Try drinking a cup of herbal tea before bed. It might help.

In the end, my suggestions were completely off base because I didn't take the time to properly understand John's situation. What I should have done was this:

John: I'm not feeling well. Lately, I've been struggling to sleep.

Me: What's going on, John?

John: I think… well… my mind is consumed with thoughts about my upcoming blood tests. They'll be here on Monday.

Me: Are you worried they might uncover some illness or disease?

John: Yes, my father died of complications from diabetes.

Me: I'm so sorry for your loss. I hope your results will be OK. You can only wait and see, right? Try to not make yourself miserable before you even know what's going on.

That approach would have been much better! And more importantly, it would have shown John that I truly cared about understanding his situation and supporting him.

Another point to consider in this lesson is that sometimes keeping silent is more beneficial than speaking up. In Maltese, there's a proverb that captures this perfectly: "Ghidt kelma u swietli mija, m'ghidt xejn u swietli mitejn" which translates to "I said one word and it was worth a hundred. I said nothing and it was worth two hundred." There are times when silence is truly the golden rule. Words carry a lot of weight, and the wrong ones can lead to misunderstandings, unnecessary arguments, and negativity. They can also escalate tension or cause emotional harm.

Ask open-ended questions like 'How can I help you?', 'How was your day?', or 'What's your dream vacation?', instead of those that only require a 'yes' or 'no' answer. Then, truly listen and seek to understand. Allow them to finish their thoughts uninterrupted. Knowing when to hold back your own words creates space for others to be heard. This simple act can empower them, providing a space to share their ideas and experiences. We've all encountered individuals who seem to relish the sound of their own voice, dominating conversations without genuinely listening.

Let's not be those people.

37.

HAVING KIDS IS A BEAUTIFUL CHALLENGE

Man, nothing prepares you for when you have a child. It has been the most transformative and beautiful experience of my life.

I must admit, I was never in a hurry to have kids. I had big dreams and aspirations, and travel plans that I wanted to fulfill before settling down. But then my wife convinced me that we would rot if we had to wait for the perfect time for having a baby, and so we decided to try. In 2017, our daughter Julie was born. As expected, the first weeks were tough. She cried and needed constant care, leaving us both feeling overwhelmed. But as humans do, we adapted and learned how to take care of this tiny human being. And just three years later, we welcomed our second beautiful daughter Elise into the world.

Reflecting on my experience, here are a few of the hundreds of lessons I have learned after becoming a parent:

- In the first few weeks, babies may seem disappointing as they mainly sleep, eat, cry and poop. But as they grow and start reacting to the world around them, it becomes all worth it when you see their first smile or hear their first laugh.

- Yes, your life will change. You may have to make adjustments and sacrifices for your children. Your time for yourself will be limited. You will sleep less. It can be challenging at times. But if you go into parenthood expecting everything else to stay the same, you are in for a rude awakening. Your priorities and daily routine will shift drastically. However, it is important to still make time for yourself amidst the chaos of parenting.

- Some of the deepest moments of joy in my life have been with my children. The unconditional love and depth of emotion that comes with being a parent is indescribable. Seeing them wake up full of energy and potential each morning fills my heart with happiness. And even though there are difficult moments, I find joy in watching them grow, learn, and experience new things.

- It's natural to yell or threaten punishment when kids misbehave. But I've learned that explaining the consequences calmly is even more effective. For example, instead of shouting "Look where you're walking!", you can say, "Pay attention on the street. Cars can't see you easily because you're small. The sidewalk is much safer." Also kids sometimes act out to get attention. By staying calm and reasoning with them, like you would with an adult (as much as possible!), you can address the behavior and show them they don't need to act up for your attention.

-   Parenthood is not for everyone, and that's okay. It is not a solution to marital issues or a guarantee of happiness. If you are not open to changing your priorities and lifestyle, then it may not be the right choice for you.

For me, becoming a parent has been the most transformative event in my life - more than marriage, leaving my childhood home, career success, or travel adventures. And while nothing can fully prepare you for the journey of parenthood, sometimes taking the leap into the unknown can lead to the greatest rewards. I can say with certainty - for me, it was worth it.

38.

YOU ARE HUMAN. YOU HAVE LIMITS.

You, a human being, are a marvel of biology and evolution. Your consciousness allows you to think critically, adapt to new situations, interact with others, produce life, and more. But amidst these amazing abilities, there are also limitations that come along with being human. They may be frustrating at times, but they are a part of what makes us human.

The popular saying "If you can dream it, you can do it" is often attributed to Walt Disney, though its origin remains uncertain. While it holds a great message of optimism and determination, it's important to recognize that it doesn't make much sense. For example, dreaming of running naked on the rings of planet Saturn is physically impossible. Dreaming of winning more Ballon d'Or football awards then Messi and you're 88 years old with arthritis … is well … a goal you should ideally give up on. Knowing our limits can help us redirect our energy into more feasible goals or find alternative solutions.

Here are just a few examples of the many limitations we have as humans:

- We cannot multitask effectively. Our brains are not capable of focusing on two high-level activities simultaneously. Attempting to do so can lead to reduced quality of work and increased stress levels. Similarly, we cannot be in two places at once. It's important to prioritize our tasks and focus on one at a time.

- Our memory is limited. It's natural to forget things now and then, especially when juggling busy schedules. However, this limitation can be frustrating when trying to remember important information or names of people we know. I suffer from this mostly when I'm at a wedding or event and I see someone I knew from a while back and I have to introduce the person to my wife BUT I COMPLETELY FORGOT THAT PERSON'S NAME! I suffer from this all the time. Taking notes and sympathetic understanding when others forget can help us cope with this limitation.

- We have finite strength and energy. It's normal to feel drained after a long day of work or unable to complete all the tasks we had planned. Being mindful of our energy levels and prioritizing tasks can help us make the most out of our limited resources. Utilizing technology and delegating tasks can also save us precious energy.

- We all get sick sometimes. Right now, I'm on antibiotics because I had a nasty throat infection and a fever last night. I spent the whole day yesterday in bed, too tired to even read a book or watch TV. When I'm sick, it makes me think about how we're all mortal and how important it is to take care of our bodies as much as we can.

- Emotions often override logic. As emotional creatures, our actions are often driven by our feelings rather than rational thought. For example, anger can easily overpower logical thinking and lead us to make impulsive decisions. Or we may do stupid things because we are in love. However, emotions can also guide us towards what truly matters to us, such as following our passions over practical job choices.

Overall, understanding and accepting our limitations can help us work with what we have and find ways to thrive within them. We are human, after all - beautifully imperfect in our own way.

39.

MEMENTO MORI

"Memento Mori" - Latin for "Remember that you are going to die." is not just a lesson, it is a vital way of living your life.

Some may find this thought sad and depressing, but in reality, it is a powerful reminder of the limited time we have on this earth. It pushes us to make the most out of every moment, to stop postponing our dreams and start working towards them now. Memento Mori encourages us to live in the present and prioritize what truly matters: relationships, purpose, growth, and memorable experiences.

When we constantly remind ourselves of our mortality, trivial matters fade away. The car our neighbor bought or the person at work who didn't greet us with a smile became insignificant. Instead, we focus our energy on spending quality time with loved ones, embarking on new adventures, trying new things, and removing toxic people from our lives.

We understand that life should be lived, not just existing.

One common question that arises when discussing Memento Mori is "Should I stop going to work, since work is tough and death could be around the corner?". We should not abandon all responsibilities and cease productivity. Rather, we should approach everything in life with intention and a sense of fulfillment. If our current job does not bring us joy and purpose, Memento Mori suggests either finding fulfillment within it or pursuing something else entirely. Mindful living is key; we are not meant to work like slaves for the rest of our lives. We should seek a balance between productivity and a fulfilling life.

In summary, Memento Mori serves as a constant reminder to make the most out of each day, to prioritize what truly matters, and to live intentionally and mindfully. It is a reminder to embrace the present moment, pursue our passions, and leave a positive impact on the world. Let us never forget the inevitability of death and use it as motivation to lead fulfilling and meaningful lives.

We only have one shot at this gift called life.

Memento Mori. Memento Vivere.

Remember that you are going to die!

Remember that you must live!

40.

AN EXAMINED LIFE IS WORTH LIVING

Just like the Memento Mori lesson, this one is about an approach to how we live. I believe that we are part of this miracle, this great mystery, where all of a sudden we start existing into this world. In time we learn how our body works, how to interact with other people and how to navigate this planet. Then we grow, we build relationships and set up our routines and habits. This is what each of us has done so far.

But there is more!

Socrates, the Greek philosopher, once said "an unexamined life is not worth living". An examined life is one where we just don't examine the surface of what life is about but go deeper into its meaning. We do that by reflecting, by questioning our beliefs, our religions, our values and look for a purpose and true fulfillment. It's about examining our life and not just going through it like a feather in the wind. This self-discovery journey has no end and it will last all of our life. It's about trying to learn about ourselves and this life as it will make us appreciate the beauty of it all and put more meaning to it.

It's about not living life on auto-pilot.

I firmly believe that people who never reflect on their actions, motivations, values, and beliefs miss out on a richer and more genuine life, one where they uncover their true desires and live with greater authenticity. However, I don't claim that people who follow their instincts are happier. As mentioned, finding balance is key. We should find a balance between self-examination and simply living this life.

So embrace the journey and, when you can, do:

Pause. Reflect. Adjust.

This is what this book is all about. These 40 lessons were some of the reflections and discoveries I found throughout my 40 years alive so far.

I hope that many of these resonated with you and I wish you the best life ever full of love, health, meaning and reflections.

Love.
Josef.

Further Reading

Thank you for taking the time to read this book. I hope it inspires you to reflect on your own life journey and empowers you as you take your next steps.

Rather than recommending specific books, I'd like to share some incredible authors whose work has profoundly impacted me. Their insights have helped me navigate life's challenges and find guidance on my own path. Perhaps they will offer similar inspiration for you:

Mark Manson

James Clear

Simon Sinek

Gary John Bishop

Amber Rae

Tony Robbins

Jen Sincero

Brené Brown

Ali Abdall

Sonja Lyubomirsky

Acknowledgments

I want to express my deepest gratitude to my wife, Maria, and our daughters, Julie and Elise, for being the cornerstones of my life. I am incredibly grateful that our paths crossed, leading me to find such a caring, intelligent, and kind-hearted partner to share this journey with.

I also want to thank my parents, Joe and Lilian, for their guidance and for providing me with both space and love throughout my life. A special thanks to my mom, whose love of self-help books indirectly sparked my own interest and immersion in this world.

To my younger brothers, Daniel and Thomas, I wanted to express my gratitude for being the best brothers anyone could ask for. You guys are not just ridiculously talented, but also amazing dads. Your commitment to your families and your unwavering support for each other is truly inspiring. As brothers, we have always had each other's backs.

To my friends and extended family, thank you for the love, care, and support you've shown me. I deeply appreciate it. Some I haven't seen in a long while but I cherish the time we spent together and the love you've shown me.

Life has also presented me with my fair share of challenging individuals, and for them, I am also grateful. Without their presence, I wouldn't have learned the valuable lessons that have shaped me. While they may have weakened me temporarily, they ultimately presented me with challenges that have made me smarter, more introspective, and more empathetic towards the good people in the world.

Finally, I want to acknowledge God/destiny/the universe/chance for giving me the opportunity to experience all that life has to offer.

About The Author

Hailing from the tiny but vibrant island nation of Malta, hidden in the heart of the Mediterranean, Josef Cauchi was born and raised. He is married to Maria and father to two beautiful girls: Julie and Elise.

A graduate of the University of Malta, Josef holds both a Bachelor of Science in Information Technology and a Master's in Film Studies. For the past two decades, he has honed his skills in the IT industry, working as a software developer, team lead, and engineering manager. It's in leadership roles that Josef discovered his true passion: guiding and mentoring others. He firmly believes that everyone possesses untapped potential, and all they might need is a nudge and some coaching to unleash it.

Driven by his creativity, Josef has explored many avenues of expression. From writing books and composing music to crafting films, online courses, plays, digital art, and photography, he's constantly trying new things. While some might call him a jack of all trades, master of none, he embraces this creative journey and is unfazed by this.

His ultimate goal? Leave the world a little brighter. In his youth, his motto roared "Let's change the world!". Now, with a more seasoned perspective, he finds joy in even the smallest positive impacts.

If you want to know more about Josef's world, head over to his websites: www.josefcauchi.com and www.meanderman.net

May your life
be filled with
unforgettable moments,
meaningful connections,
and a constant sense of
fulfillment.